DINNER IN MINUTES

Ottenheimer Publishers, Inc.

Publisher: Sally Peters
Publication Manager: Diane B. Anderson
Senior Editor: Elaine Christiansen
Senior Food Editor: Jackie Sheehan
Test Kitchen Coordinator: Pat Peterson
Circulation Specialist: Karen Goodsell
Production Coordinator: Michele Warren
Publication Secretary: Mary Thell
Food Editor: Susanne Mattison
Food Stylist: Sharon Harding
Food Stylist's Assistant: Susanne Mattison
Contributing Editor: Patricia Miller
Consulting Editor: William Monn
Home Economists: Pillsbury Publications
Nutrition Information: Pillsbury Technology
Design: Tad Ware & Company, Inc.
Photography: Studio 3

Cover Photo: Chicken Curry Stuffed Potatoes p. 25

Printed in the U.S.A.

**Reprinted by Ottenheimer Publishers, Inc.,
with permission from Classic® Cookbooks,**

CLASSIC® Pillsbury COOKBOOKS Dinner in Minutes

Crescent Garlic Toast p. 61, Vegetable Pasta Salad with Beef p. 62

Departments

Special Features

Hearty Tomato Bean Soup p. 78, Quick 'n Crunchy Cornbread Twists p.61

Apple Pear Salad p. 67

EDITOR'S Pillsbury NOTEBOOK

Good Food — *Fast*

*You **can** put dinner on the table in just 30 minutes.*

On your mark, get set, GO! Sometimes it feels like a race to put weekday dinners on the table. When time's squeezed tight, it's easy to reach for the same old standbys — carryout, frozen pizzas, or unimaginative casseroles.

Now there's help for the dinner-time pinch. We've developed this creative collection of main-meal recipes that can be prepared in just 30 minutes. In this cookbook you'll find:

- **Double-use recipes**. Make one or two or even three deliciously different meals from one basic recipe. Menus to help you turn these double-use recipes into 30-minute meals are on pages 4 and 5.
- **Dinner-at-your-fingertips pantry list**. Having groceries on hand allows you to make dinner in minutes. On pages 6 and 7, you'll find a helpful pantry list of items used in our recipes.
- **Time-saving preparation techniques**. Your microwave, stovetop, and broiler are put into service as well as tandem combinations of these cooking methods. Because cooked chicken is a popular ingredient for casseroles, salads, entrees and sandwiches, we describe how to poach chicken in the microwave on pages 18 and 19.

Save time with tandem cooking — ready to eat in 15 minutes — Chicken Curry Stuffed Potatoes p. 25.

• **Quick and easy shopping tips**. Save time — and even money — by shopping from a list and buying ingredients that are ready-to-use from the salad bar, produce section or deli.

Meals-in-minutes don't just happen. It does take some planning and preparation to be able to pull together a balanced, attractive and great-tasting dinner in minutes. To solve your dinnertime dilemma:

• **Keep menus simple**. An uncomplicated menu with a few key dishes requires less time to prepare. Menu planning can be done in detail or with a general idea for the week. It will also streamline your grocery shopping.

• **Organize your pantry**. A well-stocked pantry gives you flexibility and versatility when fixing dinner. Today's pantry includes the cupboard, refrigerator and freezer. Use your 30-minute menus to develop a workable pantry.

• **Arrange your kitchen**. Put frequently used utensils and equipment within easy reach. Organize shelves so that labels can be read at a glance.

• **Overlap tasks**. While waiting for water to boil or meat to brown, chop vegetables, open cans or set the table.

• **Make cooking a family affair**. Assign your helpers specific tasks and work areas.

• **Keep paper plates on hand**. Paper plates, napkins, and placemats are colorful, enhance meal appeal and make clean-up a snap.

Great tasting Rotini Skillet Supper p. 10

Recipe Transformation Magic

Six terrific recipes transform into 15 dynamite dinners.

Start with six basic recipes. Add a little kitchen wizardry, and *voila*! You've got sure-to-please dinners. These aren't leftovers, they're "planned overs." Serve part of these double-use recipes for a first meal and part for a second or even a third meal. Below you'll find each of the six double-use recipes planned into tempting and satisfying dinner-in-minutes menus.

Quick Pasta Sauce *p. 11*

DOUBLE USE

A versatile meat sauce that is perfect for a supper in a skillet or a main-meal sandwich.

MENU I

Rotini Skillet Supper p. 10
Crescent Garlic Toast p. 61
Tossed Green Salad
Fresh Fruit with Yogurt Dip

MENU II

Vegetable-Topped Italian Sandwiches p. 86
Sliced Fresh Fruit
Ice Cream Floats

Microwave-Poached Chicken Breasts *p. 19*

DOUBLE USE

In just minutes, you have the main ingredient for salads, sandwiches and entrees.

MENU I

Poached Chicken with Dill Cheese Sauce p. 20
Parsley Buttered Couscous p. 69
Light and Lemony Spinach Salad p. 56
Ice Cream Sundaes

MENU II

Southwest Barbecued Chicken Sandwiches p. 85
Fresh Vegetable Sticks
Tortilla Chips
Brownies

MENU III

Chicken Curry Stuffed Potatoes p. 25
Greens with Mustard Vinaigrette p. 56
Frozen Fruit Yogurt

MENU IV

Chicken Vegetable Risotto Skillet p. 23
Sliced Tomatoes
Apple Slices with Caramel Sauce

Make-Ahead Meatballs *p. 45*

DOUBLE USE

This recipe can make three deliciously different dinners.

MENU I

Meatball Green Bean Stroganoff p. 47
Summer Fruit Combo p. 73
Chocolate Chip Cookies

MENU II

Southwest-Style Meatballs p. 46
Hot Cooked Rice
Tossed Green Salad
Sherbet

MENU III

Quick Meatball Stew p. 48
Tossed Green Salad
Melon Wedges

Quick and Easy Chili *p. 16*

DOUBLE USE

One batch makes two family-pleasing suppers.

MENU I

Quick and Easy Chili p. 16
Quick 'n Crunchy Cornbread Twists p. 61
Fresh Fruit
Ice Cream Cones

MENU II

Chili Cheese Dogs p. 89
Apple Pear Salad p. 67
Carrot Sticks
Chocolate Cupcakes

Garden Vegetable Macaroni Salad *p. 62*

DOUBLE USE

Change from a side dish to a main dish by adding just one ingredient.

MENU I

Garden Vegetable Macaroni Salad p. 62
Deli Fried Chicken
Melon Wedges and Grapes

MENU II

Vegetable Macaroni Salad with Ham p. 62
Assorted Muffins
Peach or Pear Slices

Pot Roast Turkey Tenderloin *p. 26*

DOUBLE USE

Two updated, lower cholesterol variations of Grandma's slow-cooked pot roast.

MENU I

Pot Roast Turkey Tenderloin p. 26
Crusty Rolls
Pear Raspberry Cottage Cheese Salad p. 72
Apple Pie

MENU II

Biscuit-Topped Turkey Stew p. 26
Fresh Fruit and Slaw p. 72
Ice Cream 'n Cookie Sandwiches

Dinner-At-Your-Fingertips Pantry List

A shopping list for creating the perfect meal-making pantry.

Having versatile ingredients on hand gives you time-saving, meal-making flexibility. By combining items from your cupboard, refrigerator, freezer and supermarket deli, you'll be able to pull together a nutritious, delicious dinner in minutes without dashing to the store. Now that's fast food!

THE REFRIGERATOR

Dairy
- Cheese assortment
- Eggs
- Margarine or butter
- Milk
- Sour cream, yogurt

Dressings
- Assorted salad
- Mayonnaise or salad dressing

Fruits
- Bottled lemon or lime juice
- Assortment of apples, pears, nectarines, grapes

Meats
- Bacon, wieners
- Deli-sliced assortment

Pasta
- Your choice

Prepared dough
- Biscuits
- Cornbread twists
- Crescent dinner rolls
- Sweet rolls

Vegetables
- Assorted greens
- Bell pepper, broccoli
- Carrots, celery, cucumbers
- Green onions, tomatoes

THE FREEZER

Juices
- Your choice

Meats, Fish, Poultry
- Ground beef
- Thin-sliced pork chops or steaks, cooked ham cubes, Italian sausage or bratwurst
- Fish fillets, shrimp
- Chicken breasts

Vegetables
- 16-oz. bags of vegetables — broccoli, corn, green beans, peas, spinach
- 16-oz. bags of vegetable combinations
- Hash brown potatoes

THE CUPBOARD

Breads and Crackers
Your choice
Croutons or bread crumbs

Condiments
Cranberry sauce
Ketchup
Mustards (your choice)
Olives
Pickles — dill, sweet, relish
Pimientoes
Vinegars — cider or white, red wine

Fruits
Canned
Apple juice
Peaches
Pears
Pineapple
Preserves and jellies

Meat, Fish, Poultry (canned)
Beef
Chicken
Salmon
Tuna

Miscellaneous
Chopped nuts, sunflower seeds
Cornstarch
Flour
Macaroni and cheese dinner
Pancake mix
Raisins
Seeds — poppy, sesame
Vegetable or olive oil

Pasta and Rice
Your choice

Sauces
Barbecue
Hot pepper
Picante or salsa
Soy
Spaghetti
Tomato
Worcestershire

Seasonings
Dried herbs — basil, oregano, parsley, dill weed, thyme, tarragon, fennel, marjoram
Dry mixes — taco, spaghetti, gravy

Soups, Broths, Gravy
Soups — condensed cream-style, tomato, dry oriental mixes
Broth — beef, chicken
Gravy — beef

Spices
For baking — cinnamon, ginger, nutmeg, cloves
For cooking — dry mustard, poultry seasoning, chili powder, cumin, curry, paprika

Sweeteners and Syrups
Dessert toppings
Honey
Maple syrup
Sugars — brown, granulated, powdered

Vegetables
Beans — baked, chili, kidney, pinto
Chiles
Green beans
Mushrooms
Tomatoes — whole, stewed, paste
Whole kernel corn
Fresh, non-refrigerated
Garlic
Onions
Potatoes

MAIN DISHES & ENTREES

Variety and flavor let you just say "no" to dull dinners.

An added bonus for preparing dinner is tandem cooking that shaves minutes off in-the-kitchen time by combining conventional and microwave cooking. For example, when making **Chicken Curry Stuffed Potatoes**, prepare the chicken mixture on the stovetop while cooking the potatoes in the microwave. Other tandem-cooking recipes in this chapter are:

- **Garden Vegetable and Ham-Stuffed Potatoes**
- **Italian-Style Chicken Patties**
- **Turkey Rice Medley with Acorn Squash**

*Pictured: **Rotini Skillet Supper, p. 10***

Cook's Note

Kitchen Scissors

Kitchen scissors can make quick work of many kitchen tasks. Use them to:

- Cut up fresh herbs and vegetables like parsley, basil, green onions and spinach.
- Cut up canned whole tomatoes right in the can before adding them to soups and sauces.
- Cut chicken breasts in half along the breast bone before cooking them.
- Cut pizza into serving-sized pieces.
- Snip grapes into serving-sized clusters.

***Quick Pasta Sauce** plus vegetables and cooked pasta make a speedy skillet casserole. Garnish it with Parmesan cheese and parsley and serve this main dish right from the skillet.*

ROTINI SKILLET SUPPER

(pictured on p. 8)

4 oz. (1 cup) uncooked rotini (spiral macaroni)
1 tablespoon olive oil or oil
1 cup thinly sliced carrots
4 cups Quick Pasta Sauce (this page)
1 cup Green Giant® Frozen Sweet Peas (from 16-oz. pkg.)
1 (2¼-oz.) can (¼ cup) sliced ripe olives, drained
1 tablespoon freshly grated Parmesan cheese or grated Parmesan cheese
1 tablespoon chopped fresh parsley, if desired

Cook rotini to desired doneness as directed on package. Drain; rinse with hot water.

Heat oil in large skillet over medium heat. Add carrots; cook and stir 5 to 7 minutes or until carrots are tender. Stir in pasta sauce, frozen peas and olives. Reduce heat to low; simmer 5 to 8 minutes or until peas are tender. Stir in cooked rotini; simmer an additional 1 to 2 minutes or until thoroughly heated. Garnish with Parmesan cheese and parsley.
6 (1-cup) servings.

NUTRITION INFORMATION

SERVING SIZE: 1 CUP		PERCENT U.S. RDA PER SERVING	
CALORIES	290	PROTEIN	20%
PROTEIN	13 g	VITAMIN A	140%
CARBOHYDRATE	30 g	VITAMIN C	30%
FAT	14 g	THIAMINE	35%
CHOLESTEROL	30 mg	RIBOFLAVIN	15%
SODIUM	1000 mg	NIACIN	20%
POTASSIUM	670 mg	CALCIUM	8%
		IRON	20%

*In 30 minutes, you can have a rich meat sauce that tastes as if it had simmered all day. Use it in **Rotini Skillet Supper** (this page) and **Vegetable-Topped Italian Sandwiches** (p. 86), or enjoy it over cooked pasta.*

QUICK PASTA SAUCE

DOUBLE USE

1½ lb. sweet Italian sausage or ground beef
1 cup chopped onions
2 garlic cloves, minced, or 1 teaspoon chopped garlic in oil
2 (15-oz.) cans tomato sauce
2 (14½-oz.) cans Italian-style stewed tomatoes
1 tablespoon brown sugar
1 teaspoon dried oregano leaves, crushed
1 teaspoon dried basil leaves, crushed
½ teaspoon fennel seed
⅛ teaspoon cayenne pepper, if desired

If sausage comes in casing, remove casing; break up sausage. In 4-quart saucepan or Dutch oven, brown sausage, onions and garlic; drain. Stir in remaining ingredients; bring to a boil. Reduce heat to low; simmer 15 minutes, stirring occasionally. Serve over hot cooked pasta. 9 cups.

NUTRITION INFORMATION

SERVING SIZE: 1 CUP		PERCENT U.S. RDA PER SERVING	
CALORIES	250	PROTEIN	20%
PROTEIN	14 g	VITAMIN A	30%
CARBOHYDRATE	17 g	VITAMIN C	30%
FAT	15 g	THIAMINE	30%
CHOLESTEROL	44 mg	RIBOFLAVIN	10%
SODIUM	1320 mg	NIACIN	20%
POTASSIUM	780 mg	CALCIUM	6%
		IRON	15%

Green Giant® Pasta Accents® Frozen Vegetables with Pasta plus a few additional ingredients make supper a snap to prepare.

SAVORY SAUSAGE 'N PASTA

¾ lb. Polish sausage or smoked bratwurst, cut into ½-inch pieces
1 tablespoon margarine or butter
¼ cup water
1 (16-oz.) pkg. Green Giant® Creamy Cheddar Pasta Accents® Frozen Vegetables with Pasta
¼ to ⅓ cup chopped dill pickles
1 to 2 teaspoons prepared mustard

In large skillet, brown sausage in margarine; drain. Add water and frozen vegetables with pasta. Bring to a boil; stir. Reduce heat to low; cover and simmer 4 to 6 minutes or until vegetables are crisp-tender, stirring halfway through cooking. Stir in pickles and mustard. Cover and cook an additional 1 to 2 minutes to blend flavors. 4 (1¼-cup) servings.

NUTRITION INFORMATION

SERVING SIZE: 1-1/4 CUPS		PERCENT U.S. RDA PER SERVING	
CALORIES	440	PROTEIN	25%
PROTEIN	18 g	VITAMIN A	50%
CARBOHYDRATE	24 g	VITAMIN C	6%
FAT	32 g	THIAMINE	30%
CHOLESTEROL	67 mg	RIBOFLAVIN	15%
SODIUM	1370 mg	NIACIN	20%
POTASSIUM	440 mg	CALCIUM	10%
		IRON	10%

For many busy families, breakfast foods are often prepared for dinner. When that's your plan, try this new approach to pancakes and ham.

CORNCAKES AND HAM

(pictured on right)

HONEY 'N SPICE SYRUP
- **½ cup Hungry Jack® Syrup**
- **½ cup honey**
- **¼ teaspoon cinnamon**

CORNCAKES
- **1 cup Hungry Jack® Buttermilk or Extra Lights® Complete Pancake Mix**
- **¾ cup water**
- **½ cup Green Giant® Niblets® Frozen Corn (from 16-oz. pkg.), thawed, drained**
- **4 to 8 thin slices ham**

In small saucepan, combine all syrup ingredients; blend well. Heat over low heat, stirring occasionally; keep warm.*

Heat griddle to 375°F.; grease lightly with oil. In medium bowl, combine pancake mix, water and corn. Stir just until large lumps of pancake mix disappear. For each pancake, pour scant ¼ cup batter onto hot griddle. Cook 1½ minutes, turning when edges look cooked and bubbles begin to break on surface. Continue to cook 1½ minutes or until golden brown. Heat ham slices on same griddle.

To serve, place 1 pancake on each plate; top each with 1 to 2 warm ham slices and second pancake. Pour warm syrup over pancakes.
4 servings.

TIP:
* To microwave syrup, in 2-cup microwave-safe measuring cup combine all syrup ingredients; blend well. Microwave on HIGH for 1 to 2½ minutes or until thoroughly heated, stirring once halfway through cooking.

NUTRITION INFORMATION

SERVING SIZE: 1/4 OF RECIPE		PERCENT U.S. RDA PER SERVING	
CALORIES	410	PROTEIN	15%
PROTEIN	10 g	VITAMIN A	*
CARBOHYDRATE	90 g	VITAMIN C	8%
FAT	2 g	THIAMINE	25%
CHOLESTEROL	16 mg	RIBOFLAVIN	10%
SODIUM	820 mg	NIACIN	15%
POTASSIUM	220 mg	CALCIUM	10%
		IRON	10%

* Contains less than 2% of the U.S. RDA of this nutrient.

Corncakes and Ham

Many supermarkets now have cut-up fresh vegetables in salad bars and produce sections. Take advantage of this convenience to reduce the preparation time for stir-fried meals.

SALAD BAR VEGETABLE BEEF STIR-FRY

(pictured on left)

SAUCE

- **⅓ cup water**
- **1 tablespoon cornstarch**
- **2 tablespoons soy sauce**
- **2 tablespoons honey**
- **½ teaspoon ginger**
- **¼ teaspoon salt**
- **⅛ teaspoon cinnamon**

STIR-FRY

- **2 tablespoons oil**
- **¾ lb. boneless beef sirloin, slightly frozen, cut into paper-thin strips about 2x1-inch**
- **2 garlic cloves, minced, or 1 teaspoon chopped garlic in oil**
- **1½ lb. (about 6 cups) assorted cut-up fresh vegetables***

In small bowl, blend all sauce ingredients; set aside. Heat large skillet or wok over medium-high heat until hot. Add 1 tablespoon of the oil; heat until it ripples. Add beef and garlic; cook and stir 3 to 4 minutes or until browned. Remove and reserve beef and any liquid in skillet.

In same skillet over medium heat, heat remaining 1 tablespoon oil until it ripples. Add firm vegetables (broccoli, carrots, cauliflower); cook and stir 2 minutes or until vegetables are slightly limp. Add less firm vegetables (onions, green or red bell peppers); cook and stir 2 to 3 minutes. Add soft vegetables (mushrooms, bean sprouts, pea pods); cook and stir 1 to 2 minutes or until all vegetables are crisp-tender. Return beef and any liquid to skillet; stir in sauce mixture. Cook and stir until sauce is bubbly and thickened. If using tomatoes, stir in and heat until warm. Serve with hot cooked rice or Chinese noodles, if desired. 4 to 5 servings.

TIP:

* A mixture of broccoli and cauliflower florets, thinly sliced carrots, onions and mushrooms, green or red bell pepper strips, bean sprouts, pea pods and cherry tomato halves can be used.

NUTRITION INFORMATION

SERVING SIZE: 1/5 OF RECIPE		PERCENT U.S. RDA PER SERVING	
CALORIES	210	PROTEIN	25%
PROTEIN	15 g	VITAMIN A	80%
CARBOHYDRATE	18 g	VITAMIN C	90%
FAT	9 g	THIAMINE	10%
CHOLESTEROL	35 mg	RIBOFLAVIN	15%
SODIUM	560 mg	NIACIN	15%
POTASSIUM	590 mg	CALCIUM	4%
		IRON	15%

Cook's Note

Garlic

A convenient way to achieve fresh garlic flavor in recipes without chopping it is to purchase a jar of chopped garlic packed in oil. For easy substitution in recipes, one-half teaspoon of this fresh garlic product equals one clove of garlic. You'll find this product in the produce section of your supermarket. Refrigerate it after opening to maintain its freshness.

Salad Bar Vegetable Beef Stir-fry

Cook's Note

Recipe Preparation Shortcut

Ingredients such as chopped onion, chopped bell pepper or shredded cheese can be prepared ahead whenever you have a spare minute. Seal them in plastic bags; label and refrigerate up to three days. For longer storage, the chopped onion and bell pepper can be frozen up to one month. Spread the vegetable in a single layer in a shallow baking pan; cover with plastic wrap and freeze. When frozen, break into pieces; place in freezer bag or freezerproof container. When needed in a recipe, you can add the required amount of onion or bell pepper without thawing it.

*This recipe makes enough chili for two meals. Serve part of the chili with **Quick 'n Crunchy Cornbread Twists** (p. 61) and fresh fruit. For a second meal, use the remaining chili for **Chili Cheese Dogs** (p. 89).*

QUICK AND EASY CHILI

DOUBLE USE

- **2 lb. ground beef**
- **1⅓ cups chopped onions**
- **1 cup chopped green bell pepper**
- **2 (10½-oz.) cans condensed beef broth**
- **2 (8-oz.) cans tomato sauce**
- **2 (6-oz.) cans tomato paste**
- **4 (15.5-oz.) cans Green Giant® or Joan of Arc® Light or Dark Red Kidney Beans, undrained**
- **4 teaspoons chili powder**
- **½ teaspoon hot pepper sauce**

In 5-quart saucepan or Dutch oven, brown ground beef, onions and bell pepper; drain. Stir in remaining ingredients; bring to a boil. Reduce heat to low; simmer 15 to 20 minutes, stirring occasionally. 8 (1½-cup) servings.

TIP:
Chili can be frozen in freezerproof container up to 2 months.

NUTRITION INFORMATION

SERVING SIZE: 1-1/2 CUPS		PERCENT U.S. RDA PER SERVING	
CALORIES	500	PROTEIN	60%
PROTEIN	36 g	VITAMIN A	45%
CARBOHYDRATE	50 g	VITAMIN C	50%
FAT	19 g	THIAMINE	25%
CHOLESTEROL	69 mg	RIBOFLAVIN	25%
SODIUM	1910 mg	NIACIN	40%
POTASSIUM	1580 mg	CALCIUM	10%
		IRON	40%

On-hand ingredients are the key to dinner in minutes. This recipe uses such ingredients to create an easy skillet supper the whole family will enjoy.

CHEESEBURGER SKILLET DINNER

- **1 (7¼-oz.) pkg. macaroni and cheese dinner**
- **¼ cup margarine or butter**
- **¼ cup milk**
- **1 lb. ground beef or turkey**
- **½ cup chopped onion**
- **2 cups Green Giant® Frozen Mixed Vegetables (from 16-oz. pkg.)**
- **⅓ cup ketchup**
- **¼ cup water**
- **½ teaspoon prepared mustard**
- **¼ teaspoon garlic powder**
- **3 oz. (¾ cup) shredded Cheddar cheese**

Prepare macaroni and cheese dinner as directed on package. Meanwhile, in large skillet, brown ground beef and onion; drain. Stir in frozen vegetables, ketchup, water, mustard and garlic powder. Cook over medium heat 8 to 10 minutes or until vegetables are crisp-tender, stirring occasionally. Reduce heat to low. Stir in Cheddar cheese.

Add macaroni and cheese to meat mixture; mix well. Cook 1 to 2 minutes or until thoroughly heated. Sprinkle with additional Cheddar cheese, if desired. 4 (1-cup) servings.

NUTRITION INFORMATION

SERVING SIZE: 1 CUP		PERCENT U.S. RDA PER SERVING	
CALORIES	550	PROTEIN	50%
PROTEIN	31 g	VITAMIN A	110%
CARBOHYDRATE	38 g	VITAMIN C	10%
FAT	31 g	THIAMINE	15%
CHOLESTEROL	90 mg	RIBOFLAVIN	25%
SODIUM	800 mg	NIACIN	35%
POTASSIUM	640 mg	CALCIUM	25%
		IRON	20%

Cooking the peas and macaroni together saves time and equipment in this extra creamy version of tuna noodle casserole.

CREAMY TUNA MAC 'N CHEESE

- **3 cups cold water**
- **¼ cup chopped onion**
- **1 (7¼-oz.) pkg. macaroni and cheese dinner**
- **1 cup Green Giant® Frozen Sweet Peas (from 16-oz. pkg.)**
- **⅓ cup dairy sour cream**
- **¼ cup milk**
- **¼ cup margarine or butter**
- **1 (6½-oz.) can tuna, drained, flaked**
- **2 oz. (½ cup) shredded American or Cheddar cheese**

In 3-quart saucepan, combine water, onion and macaroni from macaroni and cheese dinner; bring to a boil. Reduce heat to low; cover and simmer 5 minutes. Stir in frozen peas. Cover; simmer an additional 3 to 5 minutes or until macaroni is tender; drain.

Add sour cream, milk, margarine and cheese sauce mix from macaroni and cheese dinner to cooked macaroni and peas; mix well. Stir in tuna. Cook 2 to 3 minutes or until thoroughly heated, stirring occasionally. Sprinkle with American cheese. 4 (1¼-cup) servings.

NUTRITION INFORMATION

SERVING SIZE: 1-1/4 CUPS		PERCENT U.S. RDA PER SERVING	
CALORIES	330	PROTEIN	35%
PROTEIN	22 g	VITAMIN A	15%
CARBOHYDRATE	27 g	VITAMIN C	8%
FAT	16 g	THIAMINE	20%
CHOLESTEROL	29 mg	RIBOFLAVIN	20%
SODIUM	690 mg	NIACIN	35%
POTASSIUM	340 mg	CALCIUM	20%
		IRON	15%

CLASSIC Pillsbury KNOW-HOW™

Poaching Chicken in the Microwave

A fuss-free method for cooking chicken in half the time.

When a recipe calls for cooked chicken, what could be quicker than reaching into your freezer for just the right amount! This microwave method for cooking chicken is fast, fuss-free and flavorful. It takes only a few minutes to poach eight breasts for immediate use or to store for later use in salads, sandwiches, casseroles or main dishes.

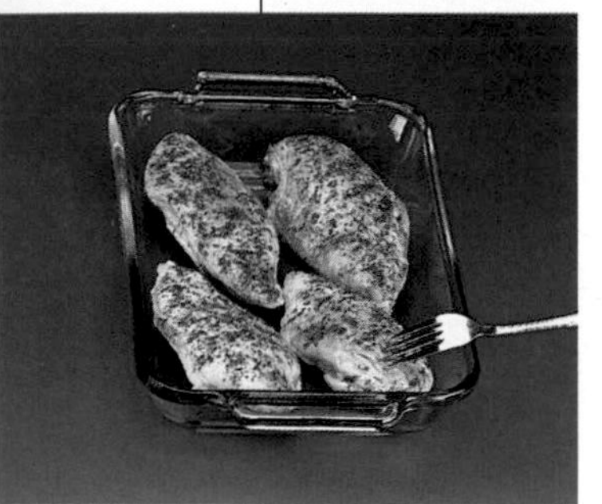

Step 1. Place four of the chicken breast halves, skin side up, in a 2-quart microwave-safe baking dish, with the thickest portions placed toward the outside edges of the dish. Sprinkle the chicken lightly with seasonings.

Step 2. Cover the dish with waxed paper.

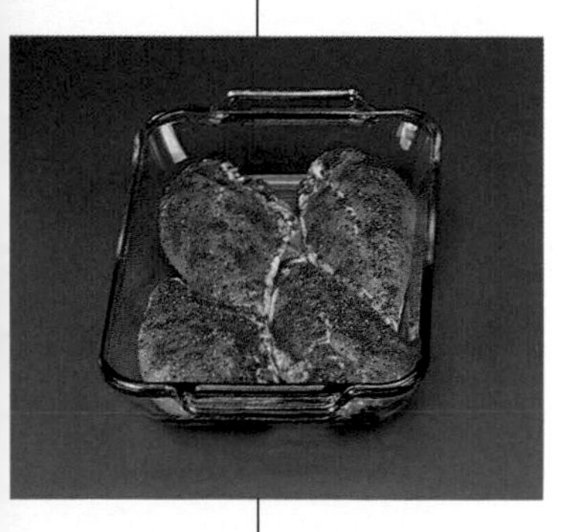

Step 3. Microwave on HIGH for 12 to 14 minutes or until the chicken is fork tender and juices run clear. Repeat with the remaining four breast halves.

Step 4. Use the chicken immediately, as shown on p. 19, or cool it completely before removing the meat from the bones. Package the cooked chicken in freezer bags or containers in amounts you will use in recipes.

Chicken can be poached quickly in the microwave to use in salads and casseroles. Chicken breasts should be about the same size to cook evenly.

MICROWAVE-POACHED CHICKEN BREASTS

DOUBLE USE

- **8 chicken breast halves (about 3 lbs.), skin removed if desired**
- **½ teaspoon seasoned salt, if desired**
- **Paprika**
- **Pepper, if desired**

MICROWAVE DIRECTIONS: Place 4 of the chicken breast halves, skin side up, in 12x8-inch (2-quart) microwave-safe baking dish, placing thickest portions toward outside edge of dish. Lightly sprinkle each breast with seasoned salt, paprika and pepper. Cover with waxed paper. Microwave on HIGH for 12 to 14 minutes or until chicken is fork tender and juices run clear, turning halfway through cooking. Repeat with remaining 4 chicken breasts. Serve warm as directed in **Poached Chicken with Dill Cheese Sauce** (p. 20), or remove chicken from bones and use as desired.
8 servings or about 4 cups cooked chicken.

TIPS:

To freeze poached chicken, cool completely. Remove chicken from bones; coarsely cut up. Place 1 to 2 cups chicken in each freezerproof container or freezer bag; label and date. Chicken can be frozen up to 2 months.

To thaw 1 to 2 cups chicken, place in 1½ to 2-quart microwave-safe casserole. Cover. Microwave on DEFROST for 4 to 6 minutes or until thawed, breaking up and rearranging chicken once halfway through thawing. (Chicken should be cool to the touch when thawed.) Or, thaw overnight in refrigerator.

NUTRITION INFORMATION

SERVING SIZE: 1/8 OF RECIPE		**PERCENT U.S. RDA PER SERVING**	
CALORIES	140	PROTEIN	40%
PROTEIN	26 g	VITAMIN A	*
CARBOHYDRATE	0 g	VITAMIN C	*
FAT	3 g	THIAMINE	4%
CHOLESTEROL	72 mg	RIBOFLAVIN	6%
SODIUM	160 mg	NIACIN	60%
POTASSIUM	220 mg	CALCIUM	*
		IRON	4%

* Contains less than 2% of the U.S. RDA of this nutrient.

Microwave-Poached Chicken Breasts, shown as Poached Chicken with Dill Cheese Sauce, p. 20

Top moist and tender chicken breasts with this scrumptious sauce.

POACHED CHICKEN WITH DILL CHEESE SAUCE

(pictured on right)

4 Microwave-Poached Chicken Breasts (page 19)

SAUCE

2 tablespoons margarine or butter
4 teaspoons flour
¼ teaspoon salt
⅛ teaspoon pepper
½ teaspoon Dijon mustard
1 cup milk
4 oz. (1 cup) shredded American or Cheddar cheese
1 teaspoon dried dill weed

MICROWAVE DIRECTIONS: Prepare chicken breasts as directed in Microwave-Poached Chicken Breasts recipe; keep warm.

Place margarine in 4-cup microwave-safe measuring cup. Microwave on HIGH for 30 to 40 seconds or until melted. Stir in flour, salt, pepper and mustard until smooth. Using wire whisk, gradually blend in milk. Microwave on HIGH for 3 to 5 minutes or until mixture thickens and boils, stirring twice during cooking. Stir in cheese and dill, stirring until cheese is melted. Spoon warm sauce over each cooked chicken breast. Serve with hot cooked pasta or rice, if desired. 4 servings.

NUTRITION INFORMATION

SERVING SIZE: 1/4 OF RECIPE		PERCENT U.S. RDA PER SERVING	
CALORIES	320	PROTEIN	50%
PROTEIN	33 g	VITAMIN A	10%
CARBOHYDRATE	8 g	VITAMIN C	*
FAT	16 g	THIAMINE	8%
CHOLESTEROL	92 mg	RIBOFLAVIN	20%
SODIUM	790 mg	NIACIN	60%
POTASSIUM	400 mg	CALCIUM	25%
		IRON	6%

* Contains less than 2% of the U.S. RDA of this nutrient.

Poached Chicken with Dill Cheese Sauce

Cook's Note

Cut-Up Cooked Chicken

Cut-up cooked chicken is convenient to have on hand for recipes. To prepare cooked chicken, we recommend poaching seasoned chicken breasts. Poaching is cooking food in a simmering liquid such as water or broth. You will find two easy methods for poaching in this cookbook — Microwave-Poached Chicken Breasts, page 19, and Skillet-Poached Chicken Breasts, this page. Use one of these methods for preparing your own cooked chicken, or look for it in the freezer section of the supermarket.

Store cut-up chicken in the refrigerator up to two days. For storage up to two months, place it in freezerproof containers or bags; label, date and freeze.

Thaw cooked chicken in a microwave-safe covered casserole. Microwave on DEFROST for 4 to 6 minutes or until thawed, breaking up and rearranging chicken halfway through thawing. When thawed, chicken should feel cool to the touch. Chicken can also be thawed in its freezerproof container overnight in the refrigerator.

Recipes in this cookbook that use cut-up chicken are:

Chicken Curry Stuffed Potatoes, page 25.

Chicken Mushroom Wild Rice Soup, page 89.

Chicken Vegetable Risotto Supper, page 23.

Enchilada-Style Chicken Pie, page 40.

Oriental Vegetable Noodle Soup, page 76.

Southwest Barbecued Chicken Sandwiches, page 85.

For additional flavor when poaching chicken, add onions and carrots to the water or poach the chicken in fruit juice.

SKILLET-POACHED CHICKEN BREASTS

8 chicken breast halves (about 3 lb.), skin removed if desired
½ teaspoon seasoned salt, if desired
Paprika
Pepper, if desired
1⅓ cups water

Lightly sprinkle skin side of each breast with seasoned salt, paprika and pepper. Place water in large skillet; bring to a boil. Add 4 of the chicken breast halves, skin side up. Reduce heat to low; cover and simmer 20 to 28 minutes or until chicken is fork tender and juices run clear. Repeat with remaining 4 chicken breasts. Serve warm or remove chicken from bones and use as desired. 8 servings or about 4 cups cooked chicken.

TIPS:

To freeze poached chicken, cool completely. Remove chicken from bones; coarsely cut up. Place 1 to 2 cups chicken in each freezerproof container or freezer bag; label and date. Chicken can be frozen up to 2 months.

To thaw 1 to 2 cups chicken, place in 1½ to 2-quart microwave-safe casserole. Cover. Microwave on DEFROST for 4 to 6 minutes or until thawed, breaking up and rearranging chicken once halfway through thawing. (Chicken should be cool to the touch when thawed.) Or, thaw overnight in refrigerator.

NUTRITION INFORMATION

SERVING SIZE: 1/8 OF RECIPE		PERCENT U.S. RDA PER SERVING	
CALORIES	140	PROTEIN	40%
PROTEIN	26 g	VITAMIN A	*
CARBOHYDRATE	0 g	VITAMIN C	*
FAT	3 g	THIAMINE	4%
CHOLESTEROL	72 mg	RIBOFLAVIN	6%
SODIUM	160 mg	NIACIN	60%
POTASSIUM	220 mg	CALCIUM	*
		IRON	4%

* Contains less than 2% of the U.S. RDA of this nutrient.

Risotto is an Italian rice specialty. Risottos can be flavored with various ingredients as in this recipe, turning this classic rice dish into a simple supper.

CHICKEN VEGETABLE RISOTTO SUPPER

2 tablespoons oil
1 cup uncooked regular rice
½ cup chopped onion
1 garlic clove, minced, or ½ teaspoon chopped garlic in oil
2½ cups chicken broth
2 cups Green Giant® American Mixtures™ Heartland Style Frozen Broccoli, Cauliflower and Carrots (from 16-oz. pkg.)
1½ cups cut-up cooked chicken
2 oz. (½ cup) freshly grated Parmesan cheese or ¼ cup grated Parmesan cheese

Heat oil in large skillet over medium-high heat. Add rice, onion and garlic; cook and stir 6 to 8 minutes or until rice is golden brown. Stir in broth; bring to a boil. Reduce heat to low; cover and simmer 15 to 20 minutes or until liquid is absorbed.

Meanwhile, cook vegetables until crisp-tender as directed on package; drain. Add cooked vegetables and chicken to rice mixture. Cook and stir 2 to 3 minutes or until thoroughly heated. Add Parmesan cheese; mix well. Sprinkle each serving with additional Parmesan cheese, if desired. 7 (1-cup) servings.

NUTRITION INFORMATION

SERVING SIZE: 1 CUP		PERCENT U.S. RDA PER SERVING	
CALORIES	250	PROTEIN	25%
PROTEIN	16 g	VITAMIN A	30%
CARBOHYDRATE	26 g	VITAMIN C	25%
FAT	9 g	THIAMINE	10%
CHOLESTEROL	32 mg	RIBOFLAVIN	8%
SODIUM	450 mg	NIACIN	25%
POTASSIUM	310 mg	CALCIUM	10%
		IRON	10%

Great-tasting convenience foods team up for a fast dinner. Serve this with a tossed green salad and garlic toast.

ITALIAN-STYLE CHICKEN PATTIES

1 (12-oz.) pkg. frozen breaded chicken breast patties
2 (4x4-inch) slices mozzarella cheese, cut in half
1 (14-oz.) jar prepared spaghetti sauce

MICROWAVE DIRECTIONS: Microwave chicken patties as directed on package. Place cheese slice on each patty. Microwave on HIGH an additional 1 to 2 minutes or until cheese is melted.

Place spaghetti sauce in 4-cup microwave-safe measuring cup or bowl. Cover with waxed paper. Microwave on HIGH for 4 to 5 minutes or until thoroughly heated, stirring once halfway through cooking. To serve, spoon warm sauce over each patty. 4 servings.

CONVENTIONAL DIRECTIONS: Bake chicken patties as directed on package. Place cheese slice on each patty. Bake an additional 1 to 2 minutes or until cheese is melted.

Meanwhile, heat spaghetti sauce in small saucepan over low heat, stirring occasionally. To serve, spoon warm sauce over each patty.

TIP:
For tandem cooking, prepare chicken patties according to microwave directions. Meanwhile, heat spaghetti sauce according to conventional directions.

NUTRITION INFORMATION

SERVING SIZE: 1/4 OF RECIPE		PERCENT U.S. RDA PER SERVING	
CALORIES	420	PROTEIN	35%
PROTEIN	23 g	VITAMIN A	25%
CARBOHYDRATE	28 g	VITAMIN C	15%
FAT	24 g	THIAMINE	8%
CHOLESTEROL	42 mg	RIBOFLAVIN	15%
SODIUM	1420 mg	NIACIN	30%
POTASSIUM	550 mg	CALCIUM	15%
		IRON	10%

This tater topping includes flavors reminiscent of a favorite midwestern casserole. It's a delicious, quick and satisfying dinner idea.

CHICKEN CURRY STUFFED POTATOES

(pictured on left)

4 medium baking potatoes, scrubbed
2 cups Green Giant® Frozen Cut Broccoli (from 16-oz. pkg.)
¼ cup chopped red bell pepper
1 cup chicken broth
2 tablespoons flour
½ teaspoon curry powder
¼ teaspoon onion salt
1 cup dairy sour cream
2 teaspoons lemon juice
1 cup cut-up cooked chicken
2 oz. (½ cup) shredded Cheddar cheese

MICROWAVE DIRECTIONS:
Pierce potatoes with fork; place on microwave-safe roasting rack. Microwave on HIGH for 5 minutes; turn potatoes. Microwave on HIGH an additional 5 to 7 minutes or until tender; keep warm.

Cook broccoli and peppers as directed on package in 2-quart microwave-safe casserole; drain.

In 4-cup microwave-safe measuring cup using wire whisk, blend broth, flour, curry powder and onion salt. Microwave on HIGH for 3½ to 4½ minutes or until mixture thickens and boils, stirring once halfway through cooking. Stir in sour cream, lemon juice and chicken. Add to cooked broccoli; mix well. Microwave on HIGH for 3 to 4 minutes or until thoroughly heated, stirring once halfway through cooking.

Cut potatoes in half lengthwise, cutting to but not through bottom of potatoes. Mash slightly with fork. Place each on plate; spoon chicken mixture evenly oven potatoes. Sprinkle each with cheese.
4 servings.

CONVENTIONAL DIRECTIONS:
Heat oven to 400°F. Pierce potatoes with fork. Bake at 400°F. for 45 to 55 minutes or until tender.

Meanwhile, in small bowl using wire whisk, blend broth, flour, curry powder and onion salt. Heat **1 tablespoon oil** in large skillet over medium-high heat. Gradually add frozen broccoli and peppers; cook and stir 5 to 7 minutes or until broccoli is crisp-tender. Reduce heat to medium. Gradually stir in chicken broth mixture; cook and stir until sauce is bubbly and thickened. Remove from heat. Stir in sour cream, lemon juice and chicken. Cook over low heat 2 minutes or until thoroughly heated. Serve as directed above.

TIP:
For tandem cooking, prepare potatoes according to microwave directions. Meanwhile, prepare chicken mixture according to conventional directions.

NUTRITION INFORMATION

SERVING SIZE: 1/4 OF RECIPE		**PERCENT U.S. RDA PER SERVING**	
CALORIES	520	PROTEIN	40%
PROTEIN	25 g	VITAMIN A	40%
CARBOHYDRATE	62 g	VITAMIN C	60%
FAT	21 g	THIAMINE	20%
CHOLESTEROL	73 mg	RIBOFLAVIN	20%
SODIUM	480 mg	NIACIN	40%
POTASSIUM	1320 mg	CALCIUM	25%
		IRON	25%

Chicken Curry Stuffed Potatoes

We've used fresh turkey in this recipe as a quick-cooking alternative to beef pot roast.

POT ROAST TURKEY TENDERLOIN

DOUBLE USE
(pictured on right)

1 tablespoon margarine or butter
2 lb. fresh turkey tenderloins, cut into 1½x1½-inch pieces
1 (12-oz.) jar prepared brown gravy
1 (8-oz.) can tomato sauce
⅛ teaspoon pepper
4 medium carrots, cut into 1-inch pieces, halved lengthwise
2 medium potatoes, scrubbed, cut into 1½-inch pieces
2 medium onions, quartered
2 cups (8 oz.) fresh mushrooms, quartered
1 tablespoon flour
2 tablespoons cold water

Melt margarine in 5-quart saucepan or Dutch oven over medium-high heat. Add turkey; cook 3 minutes on each side or until browned. Stir in gravy, tomato sauce and pepper. Add carrots, potatoes, onions and mushrooms. Reduce heat to medium-low; cover and simmer 15 to 20 minutes or until turkey and vegetables are tender, stirring occasionally.

In small jar with tight-fitting lid, combine flour and water; shake well. Gradually stir into turkey mixture; cook until thickened, stirring frequently. If desired, sprinkle with chopped fresh parsley.
6 (1½-cup) servings.

NUTRITION INFORMATION

SERVING SIZE: 1-1/2 CUPS		PERCENT U.S. RDA PER SERVING	
CALORIES	350	PROTEIN	80%
PROTEIN	51 g	VITAMIN A	280%
CARBOHYDRATE	25 g	VITAMIN C	20%
FAT	5 g	THIAMINE	15%
CHOLESTEROL	127 mg	RIBOFLAVIN	25%
SODIUM	670 mg	NIACIN	70%
POTASSIUM	1130 mg	CALCIUM	4%
		IRON	20%

A cheesy biscuit topping transforms "planned-over" ***Pot Roast Turkey Tenderloin*** *into a hearty stew.*

BISCUIT-TOPPED TURKEY STEW

(pictured on right)

BISCUITS
1 (10-oz.) can Hungry Jack® Refrigerated Flaky Biscuits
1 tablespoon margarine or butter, melted
2 tablespoons grated Parmesan cheese
Paprika

STEW
5 cups prepared Pot Roast Turkey Tenderloin (this page)
1 cup Green Giant® Frozen Sweet Peas (from 16-oz. pkg.)

Heat oven to 400°F. Separate dough into 10 biscuits. Using scissors, cut each into 4 pieces; place on ungreased cookie sheet. Brush with margarine; sprinkle with Parmesan cheese and paprika. Bake at 400°F. for 6 to 9 minutes or until golden brown. Immediately remove from cookie sheet.

Meanwhile, in large saucepan combine turkey mixture and frozen peas. Cook over medium-low heat 5 to 10 minutes or until thoroughly heated and peas are tender, stirring occasionally. To serve, spoon turkey mixture into bowls; top each serving with biscuits. 4 (1¼-cup) servings.

NUTRITION INFORMATION

SERVING SIZE: 1-1/4 CUPS		PERCENT U.S. RDA PER SERVING	
CALORIES	560	PROTEIN	70%
PROTEIN	48 g	VITAMIN A	240%
CARBOHYDRATE	53 g	VITAMIN C	25%
FAT	17 g	THIAMINE	30%
CHOLESTEROL	108 mg	RIBOFLAVIN	35%
SODIUM	1390 mg	NIACIN	70%
POTASSIUM	1060 mg	CALCIUM	10%
		IRON	30%

Pot Roast Turkey Tenderloin, Biscuit-Topped Turkey Stew

Lightly sweetened acorn squash slices provide a tasty, colorful background for the savory turkey-rice topping in this recipe. To reduce cooking time, microwave the squash.

TURKEY RICE MEDLEY WITH ACORN SQUASH

(pictured on left)

3 tablespoons margarine or butter
3 tablespoons Hungry Jack® Syrup or honey
¼ teaspoon salt
⅛ teaspoon ginger
1 medium (1½-lb.) acorn squash, cut in half lengthwise, seeds removed
¾ lb. ground turkey
⅓ cup chopped onion
2 (10-oz.) pkg. Green Giant® Rice Originals® Frozen Rice Medley, thawed
⅓ cup raisins
2 oz. (½ cup) shredded Swiss cheese

MICROWAVE DIRECTIONS:
In small microwave-safe bowl, combine margarine, syrup, salt and ginger. Microwave on HIGH for 30 to 40 seconds or until margarine is melted; blend well. Set aside.

Cut squash halves crosswise into 1-inch thick slices. Arrange slices in 12x8-inch (2-quart) microwave-safe baking dish. Cover with microwave-safe plastic wrap. Microwave on HIGH for 5 to 10 minutes or until squash is tender, rotating dish ½ turn halfway through cooking. Pour margarine mixture over squash. Cover; let stand 5 minutes.

In 2-quart microwave-safe casserole, combine turkey and onion. Microwave on HIGH for 4 to 5 minutes or until turkey is no longer pink, stirring and breaking up large pieces of turkey once halfway through cooking. Drain. Stir in rice mixture and raisins. Microwave on HIGH for 4 to 5 minutes or until thoroughly heated, stirring once halfway through cooking. Stir in cheese.

To serve, place 2 squash slices on each plate. Spoon margarine mixture from squash over slices. Spoon about ¾ cup turkey mixture over squash. 5 servings.

CONVENTIONAL DIRECTIONS:
Heat oven to 375°F. In small saucepan, combine margarine, syrup, salt and ginger. Cook over low heat until margarine is melted; blend well. Set aside.

Cut squash halves crosswise into 1-inch thick slices. Arrange slices in ungreased 12x8-inch (2-quart) baking dish; cover. Bake at 375°F. for 30 to 35 minutes or until almost tender. Pour margarine mixture over squash; cover. Bake an additional 10 minutes or until squash is tender.

Meanwhile, lightly grease large skillet. Add turkey and onion; cook and stir over medium-high heat 5 to 7 minutes or until turkey is no longer pink. Drain if necessary. Stir in rice mixture and raisins. Reduce heat to medium; cook 5 minutes or until thoroughly heated, stirring occasionally. Remove from heat; stir in cheese. Serve as directed above.

TIP:
For tandem cooking, prepare squash according to microwave directions. Meanwhile, prepare turkey mixture according to conventional directions.

NUTRITION INFORMATION

SERVING SIZE: 1/5 OF RECIPE		**PERCENT U.S. RDA PER SERVING**	
CALORIES	410	PROTEIN	30%
PROTEIN	20 g	VITAMIN A	90%
CARBOHYDRATE	45 g	VITAMIN C	20%
FAT	18 g	THIAMINE	25%
CHOLESTEROL	44 mg	RIBOFLAVIN	10%
SODIUM	570 mg	NIACIN	25%
POTASSIUM	650 mg	CALCIUM	20%
		IRON	15%

Turkey Rice Medley with Acorn Squash

A simple topping of vegetables, meat and cheese makes these baked potatoes a light and satisfying main dish.

GARDEN VEGETABLE AND HAM-STUFFED POTATOES

4 medium baking potatoes, scrubbed
1 tablespoon margarine or butter
1 cup sliced fresh mushrooms
2 cups coarsely chopped fresh spinach
1 cup chopped cooked ham
½ cup cubed tomato
¼ teaspoon seasoned salt or garlic salt
Dash pepper
8 oz. (2 cups) shredded colby/Monterey jack blend cheese or colby cheese

MICROWAVE DIRECTIONS:
Pierce potatoes with fork; place on microwave-safe roasting rack. Microwave on HIGH for 5 minutes; turn potatoes. Microwave on HIGH an additional 5 to 7 minutes or until tender; keep warm.

Place margarine in 2-quart microwave-safe casserole or large bowl. Microwave on HIGH for 30 to 45 seconds or until melted. Stir in mushrooms. Microwave on HIGH for 45 to 60 seconds or until mushrooms are thoroughly heated. Add spinach, ham, tomato, salt and pepper; toss lightly. Microwave on HIGH for 1½ to 2½ minutes or until spinach is wilted, stirring once halfway through cooking.

Cut potatoes in half lengthwise, cutting to but not through bottom of potatoes. Mash slightly with fork. Place each on plate; sprinkle with cheese. Using slotted spoon, divide vegetable mixture evenly over potatoes. 4 servings.

CONVENTIONAL DIRECTIONS:
Heat oven to 400°F. Pierce potatoes with fork. Bake at 400°F. for 45 to 55 minutes or until tender.

Meanwhile, melt margarine in large skillet over medium heat. Add mushrooms; cook and stir until mushrooms are thoroughly heated. Add spinach, ham, tomato, salt and pepper; toss lightly. Cook and stir 2 to 3 minutes or until spinach is wilted. Serve as directed above.

TIP:
For tandem cooking, prepare potatoes according to microwave directions. Meanwhile, prepare vegetable mixture according to conventional directions.

NUTRITION INFORMATION

SERVING SIZE: 1/4 OF RECIPE		PERCENT U.S. RDA PER SERVING	
CALORIES	530	PROTEIN	40%
PROTEIN	27 g	VITAMIN A	50%
CARBOHYDRATE	55 g	VITAMIN C	50%
FAT	23 g	THIAMINE	35%
CHOLESTEROL	70 mg	RIBOFLAVIN	30%
SODIUM	940 mg	NIACIN	30%
POTASSIUM	1280 mg	CALCIUM	45%
		IRON	25%

This delicious barbecued pork is made in just 20 minutes, but it tastes like it has simmered for hours.

SKILLET BARBECUED PORK CHOPS

½ teaspoon garlic powder
½ teaspoon ginger
⅛ teaspoon pepper
4 (½-inch thick) pork loin chops or steaks
1 tablespoon oil
½ cup chili sauce or ketchup
¼ cup soy sauce
2 tablespoons honey

In small bowl, combine garlic powder, ginger and pepper; blend well. Sprinkle mixture on both sides of pork chops. (Reserve any remaining garlic powder mixture.) Heat oil in large skillet over medium heat. Add pork chops; cook 2 to 3 minutes on each side or until browned.

In small bowl, combine chili sauce, soy sauce, honey and any remaining garlic powder mixture; blend well. Pour over pork chops. Reduce heat to low; cover and simmer 10 to 15 minutes or until pork chops are tender. Serve with hot cooked rice or potatoes, if desired. 4 servings.

NUTRITION INFORMATION

SERVING SIZE: 1/4 OF RECIPE		PERCENT U.S. RDA PER SERVING	
CALORIES	270	PROTEIN	30%
PROTEIN	20 g	VITAMIN A	10%
CARBOHYDRATE	19 g	VITAMIN C	6%
FAT	13 g	THIAMINE	40%
CHOLESTEROL	62 mg	RIBOFLAVIN	15%
SODIUM	1530 mg	NIACIN	25%
POTASSIUM	420 mg	CALCIUM	*
		IRON	8%

* Contains less than 2% of the U.S. RDA of this nutrient.

Cook's Note

Planning Menus

Menu suggestions and recipes throughout this cookbook can embellish your own creative ideas for wholesome, tasty meals your family and guests will enjoy. Using these few simple guidelines, menu planning will be easier, quicker and more rewarding for you.

- Begin with a main dish for each meal and then add appropriate side dishes.
- Plan two- or three-course meals, using purchased items as well as foods you prepare.
- Variety is the key to an appealing meal or week's menus. Vary food flavors, colors, textures and temperatures to create interesting contrasts. Add garnishes for interest.
- Expand your usual menu repertoire with new recipes from cookbooks, magazines or friends.
- Introduce ethnic foods for a change of pace or have an occasional theme dinner.
- Vary menus to suit the season.
- Be realistic about the amount of time you have for meal preparation. Choose quick-to-fix foods for busy days and more elaborate dishes when time is available. Plan meals that can be quickly reheated in the microwave for days when family members eat at different times. Incorporate double-use recipes (see Index) into a week's menu plan.
- Keep your menu lists to reuse by mixing and matching recipes in later weeks.

RECIPE Pillsbury MAKE-OVER

Fast, Flavorful Fish Fillets

Less time, less fat, great taste — what could be better!

Pan-fried or microwave-cooked, fish fillets make a tasty, quick-to-fix meal. **Pan-Fried Fish** is our original or traditional recipe for pan frying fish. **Easy Breaded Fish Fillets** are cooked in the microwave with no additional fat so they are lower in fat and calories. The crushed crouton coating on **Easy Breaded Fish Fillets** keeps the fish moist and flaky and gives the crisp texture everyone likes in breaded fried fish.

Easy Breaded Fish Fillets

RECIPE MAKE-OVER

This breading mixture creates a light crispy coating for fish prepared in the microwave or oven.

EASY BREADED FISH FILLETS

(pictured on p. 32)

¾ cup crushed seasoned croutons
¼ cup grated Parmesan cheese
2 teaspoons dried parsley flakes
¼ teaspoon paprika
1 egg
1 tablespoon water
1 tablespoon lemon juice
1 lb. fresh or frozen fish fillets, thawed

MICROWAVE DIRECTIONS:
In shallow dish, combine croutons, Parmesan cheese, parsley flakes and paprika; blend well. In another shallow dish, combine egg, water and lemon juice; blend well.

Cut fish into 2½ to 3-inch pieces. Dip in egg mixture; coat with crouton mixture. Tuck thin ends of fish under to form pieces of uniform thickness.* Place half of the fish on microwave-safe roasting rack. Microwave on HIGH for 3 to 3½ minutes or until fish flakes easily with fork, rotating rack once halfway through cooking. Place fish on serving plate; keep warm. Repeat with remaining fish pieces. 4 servings.

TIPS:
* Fish pieces of the same size and thickness will cook more evenly. If fillets are quite thin, put 2 fillets together.

To bake fish in conventional oven, prepare as directed above. Bake at 350°F. for 10 to 15 minutes or until fish flakes easily with fork.

NUTRITION INFORMATION

SERVING SIZE: 1/4 OF RECIPE		PERCENT U.S. RDA PER SERVING	
CALORIES	210	PROTEIN	40%
PROTEIN	27 g	VITAMIN A	6%
CARBOHYDRATE	9 g	VITAMIN C	2%
FAT	5 g	THIAMINE	6%
CHOLESTEROL	110 mg	RIBOFLAVIN	8%
SODIUM	390 mg	NIACIN	10%
POTASSIUM	270 mg	CALCIUM	10%
		IRON	4%

ORIGINAL RECIPE

This traditional method of preparing fish remains a favorite.

PAN-FRIED FISH

1 egg, slightly beaten
¼ cup milk
½ cup Pillsbury's BEST® All Purpose or Unbleached Flour or cornmeal
1 lb. fresh or frozen fish fillets, thawed
¼ cup oil or shortening

In shallow dish, combine egg and milk; blend well. Place flour in another shallow dish. Dip fish in egg mixture; coat with flour.

Heat oil in large skillet over medium-high heat. Add fish; cook 5 to 7 minutes or until golden brown and fish flakes easily with fork, turning once during cooking. Salt and pepper to taste, if desired. 4 servings.

NUTRITION INFORMATION

SERVING SIZE: 1/4 OF RECIPE		PERCENT U.S. RDA PER SERVING	
CALORIES	290	PROTEIN	35%
PROTEIN	23 g	VITAMIN A	2%
CARBOHYDRATE	13 g	VITAMIN C	*
FAT	16 g	THIAMINE	15%
CHOLESTEROL	101 mg	RIBOFLAVIN	15%
SODIUM	90 mg	NIACIN	15%
POTASSIUM	260 mg	CALCIUM	4%
		IRON	6%

* Contains less than 2% of the U.S. RDA of this nutrient.

Fresh thyme enhances the mild flavor of the fish fillets. It can be purchased year-round in the produce section of large supermarkets.

MICROWAVED SOLE WITH LEMON HERB SAUCE

1 cup thin julienne-sliced carrots
2 tablespoons water
1 lb. fresh or frozen sole or flounder fillets, thawed
2 julienne-sliced green onions
1 tablespoon margarine or butter, melted
1 tablespoon lemon juice
1 teaspoon chopped fresh thyme or ¼ teaspoon dried thyme leaves, crushed
½ teaspoon salt

MICROWAVE DIRECTIONS: Place carrots and water in 1-quart microwave-safe casserole; cover. Microwave on HIGH for 3 to 4 minutes or until carrots are almost crisp-tender; drain. Place fish fillets in 12x8-inch or 8-inch square (2-quart) microwave-safe baking dish. Arrange carrots and green onions over fish.

In small bowl, combine margarine and lemon juice; drizzle over fish and vegetables. Sprinkle with thyme. Cover with microwave-safe plastic wrap. Microwave on HIGH for 5 to 6 minutes or until fish flakes easily with fork, rotating dish ¼ turn halfway through cooking. Sprinkle with salt. 4 servings.

CONVENTIONAL DIRECTIONS: Heat oven to 350°F. In small saucepan, bring carrots and **¼ cup water** to a boil. Reduce heat to low; simmer 3 to 4 minutes or until carrots are almost crisp-tender; drain. Place fish in ungreased 12x8-inch or 8-inch square (2-quart) baking dish. Arrange carrots and green onions over fish.

In small bowl, combine margarine and lemon juice; drizzle over fish and vegetables. Sprinkle with thyme. Cover with foil. Bake at 350°F. for 15 to 20 minutes or until fish flakes easily with fork. Sprinkle with salt.

NUTRITION INFORMATION

SERVING SIZE: 1/4 OF RECIPE		**PERCENT U.S. RDA PER SERVING**	
CALORIES	140	PROTEIN	30%
PROTEIN	20 g	VITAMIN A	180%
CARBOHYDRATE	4 g	VITAMIN C	6%
FAT	4 g	THIAMINE	6%
CHOLESTEROL	55 mg	RIBOFLAVIN	6%
SODIUM	400 mg	NIACIN	10%
POTASSIUM	410 mg	CALCIUM	2%
		IRON	2%

Because fish cooks so quickly, it is an excellent choice for last minute meals. The microwave version will get you out of the kitchen even faster!

FISH FILLETS AU GRATIN

- **1 lb. fresh or frozen fish fillets, thawed**
- **1 tablespoon lemon juice**
- **1 tablespoon chopped fresh parsley or 1 teaspoon dried parsley flakes**
- **½ teaspoon onion salt**
- **½ teaspoon paprika**
- **¼ teaspoon pepper**
- **2 oz. (½ cup) shredded American cheese**

Heat oven to 350°F. Place fish fillets in ungreased 12x8-inch or 8-inch square (2-quart) baking dish; sprinkle with lemon juice, parsley, onion salt, paprika and pepper. Bake at 350°F. for 15 to 20 minutes or until fish flakes easily with fork. Sprinkle cheese over fish. Bake an additional 1 to 2 minutes or until cheese is melted. 4 servings.

MICROWAVE DIRECTIONS: Place fish fillets in 12x8-inch or 8-inch square (2-quart) microwave-safe baking dish; sprinkle with lemon juice, parsley, onion salt, paprika and pepper. Cover tightly. Microwave on HIGH for 7 to 9 minutes or until fish flakes easily with fork, rearranging fish once halfway through cooking. Remove cover; drain well. Sprinkle with cheese; microwave on HIGH for 45 to 60 seconds or until cheese is melted.

NUTRITION INFORMATION

SERVING SIZE: 1/4 OF RECIPE		PERCENT U.S. RDA PER SERVING	
CALORIES	150	PROTEIN	35%
PROTEIN	23 g	VITAMIN A	8%
CARBOHYDRATE	1 g	VITAMIN C	2%
FAT	5 g	THIAMINE	4%
CHOLESTEROL	61 mg	RIBOFLAVIN	6%
SODIUM	470 mg	NIACIN	10%
POTASSIUM	250 mg	CALCIUM	10%
		IRON	2%

Cook's Note

Testing Fish for Doneness

Fish cooks quickly and is therefore easy to overcook. Our recipes say to cook fish until the flesh turns from translucent to opaque or white, is firm but moist, and flakes easily with a fork. To test for doneness, insert the fork tines into the thickest portion of the fish and twist gently. If the fish resists flaking and still looks translucent, continue cooking it.

A guide for determining the cooking time for fish cooked by any method other than microwaving is to allow 10 minutes for each inch of thickness. Measure the thickest part of the fish, whether whole steak, fillet, rolled or stuffed. Because fish cooks quickly, it's a good idea to set a timer.

Fresh pastas cook very quickly and are now readily available in many supermarkets.

SHRIMP AND VEGETABLES WITH FETTUCINE

(pictured above)

1 (9-oz.) pkg. refrigerated uncooked fettucine

SAUCE

1 (10¾-oz.) can condensed cream of shrimp soup
½ cup milk
½ cup dairy sour cream
½ teaspoon curry powder

SHRIMP AND VEGETABLES

2 tablespoons oil
1 (16-oz.) pkg. Green Giant® American Mixtures™ California Style Frozen Cauliflower, Carrots and Asparagus
1 (12-oz.) pkg. frozen uncooked medium shrimp, thawed
1 garlic clove, minced, or ½ teaspoon chopped garlic in oil
3 green onions, cut diagonally into 1-inch pieces

Shrimp and Vegetables with Fettucine

Cook fettucine to desired doneness as directed on package. Drain; rinse with hot water. Keep warm.

Meanwhile, in medium bowl blend all sauce ingredients; set aside. Heat oil in large skillet over medium-high heat. Gradually add frozen vegetables; cook and stir 5 to 7 minutes or until vegetables are almost tender. Add shrimp and garlic; cook and stir 3 to 4 minutes or until shrimp are light pink and vegetables are crisp-tender.

Reduce heat to low. Stir in green onions and sauce mixture; cook until thoroughly heated, stirring frequently. To serve, spoon shrimp mixture over fettucine.
4 (1¼-cup) servings.

NUTRITION INFORMATION

SERVING SIZE: 1-1/4 CUPS		PERCENT U.S. RDA PER SERVING	
CALORIES	500	PROTEIN	50%
PROTEIN	31 g	VITAMIN A	190%
CARBOHYDRATE	51 g	VITAMIN C	45%
FAT	19 g	THIAMINE	40%
CHOLESTEROL	238 mg	RIBOFLAVIN	30%
SODIUM	880 mg	NIACIN	30%
POTASSIUM	670 mg	CALCIUM	15%
		IRON	30%

Mixed vegetables add color and texture to this adaptation of a 33rd BAKE-OFF® Contest recipe.

COLORFUL CHICKEN FRIED RICE

¼ cup ketchup
2 tablespoons soy sauce
1 teaspoon ginger
½ teaspoon salt
⅛ teaspoon pepper
2 whole chicken breasts, skinned, boned, cut into thin bite-sized pieces
1 tablespoon oil or margarine
2 garlic cloves, minced, or 1 teaspoon chopped garlic in oil
2 cups Green Giant® Frozen Mixed Vegetables (from 16-oz. pkg.), thawed, drained
¼ cup finely chopped onion
1 (8-oz.) can pineapple chunks, drained
2 cups cooked rice

In medium bowl, combine ketchup, soy sauce, ginger, salt and pepper; blend well. Add chicken; stir to coat. Set aside.

Heat oil in large skillet over medium heat. Add garlic; cook and stir until light golden brown. Add chicken mixture; cook and stir 3 to 5 minutes or until chicken is no longer pink. Add mixed vegetables, onion and pineapple; cook and stir 3 to 4 minutes or until vegetables are crisp-tender. Add rice; cook and stir 1 to 2 minutes or until rice is thoroughly heated.
6 (1-cup) servings.

NUTRITION INFORMATION

SERVING SIZE: 1 CUP		PERCENT U.S. RDA PER SERVING	
CALORIES	270	PROTEIN	35%
PROTEIN	22 g	VITAMIN A	70%
CARBOHYDRATE	34 g	VITAMIN C	10%
FAT	5 g	THIAMINE	15%
CHOLESTEROL	49 mg	RIBOFLAVIN	8%
SODIUM	730 mg	NIACIN	50%
POTASSIUM	410 mg	CALCIUM	4%
		IRON	10%

Shop for bean sprouts that are fresh, crisp and pale ivory or beige in color.

GOLDEN PORK CHOW MEIN

1 tablespoon oil
1½ lb. lean pork steak, cut into ¼-inch slices
1 cup sliced carrots
½ cup diagonally sliced celery
1 cup water
2 tablespoons soy sauce
2 teaspoons sugar
1 teaspoon beef-flavor instant bouillon
½ teaspoon garlic powder
½ teaspoon grated gingerroot or ⅛ teaspoon ground ginger
8 to 9 oz. (4 cups) fresh bean sprouts
½ cup diagonally sliced green onions
1 (2-oz.) jar sliced pimiento, drained
2 tablespoons cornstarch
¼ cup cold water
Chow mein noodles

Heat oil in large skillet or wok over high heat. Add pork; cook and stir until browned. Remove and reserve pork and any liquid in skillet. Add carrots, celery, water, soy sauce, sugar, bouillon, garlic powder and gingerroot; mix well. Cover; simmer 4 to 5 minutes or until vegetables are crisp-tender. Stir in cooked pork, bean sprouts, green onions and pimiento.

In small bowl, stir cornstarch into water until dissolved. Gradually stir into vegetables. Cook and stir over medium-high heat until sauce is bubbly and thickened. Serve over chow mein noodles. 6 servings.

NUTRITION INFORMATION

SERVING SIZE: 1/6 OF RECIPE		PERCENT U.S. RDA PER SERVING	
CALORIES	340	PROTEIN	30%
PROTEIN	19 g	VITAMIN A	120%
CARBOHYDRATE	24 g	VITAMIN C	25%
FAT	19 g	THIAMINE	35%
CHOLESTEROL	58 mg	RIBOFLAVIN	25%
SODIUM	560 mg	NIACIN	25%
POTASSIUM	450 mg	CALCIUM	2%
		IRON	15%

A frittata is a flat Italian omelet that has a firmer texture than other omelets. For cooking success, evenly distribute the eggs and cook them slowly over low heat.

BACON TOMATO FRITTATA

- **6 slices bacon**
- **7 eggs**
- **¼ cup milk**
- **1 teaspoon Dijon mustard**
- **1 cup cubed seeded tomato**
- **1 garlic clove, minced, or ½ teaspoon chopped garlic in oil**
- **4 oz. (1 cup) shredded Cheddar cheese**

Cook bacon in large skillet until crisp; remove bacon, reserving 1 tablespoon drippings. Break bacon into bite-sized pieces; set aside.

In medium bowl, combine eggs, milk and mustard; blend well. Heat reserved drippings in skillet over low heat. Add tomato and garlic; cook 2 minutes or until tomato is warm, stirring frequently. Stir in bacon. Pour egg mixture into skillet; cook over low heat 4 minutes. As edges set, run spatula around edge of skillet and lift egg mixture to allow uncooked egg to flow to bottom of skillet. Cover; cook an additional 4 to 5 minutes or until top is set but still moist. Sprinkle with cheese; cover tightly. Remove from heat. Let stand 1 to 2 minutes or until cheese is melted. Cut into wedges to serve. 4 to 5 servings.

NUTRITION INFORMATION

SERVING SIZE: 1/5 OF RECIPE		PERCENT U.S. RDA PER SERVING	
CALORIES	280	PROTEIN	25%
PROTEIN	17 g	VITAMIN A	20%
CARBOHYDRATE	4 g	VITAMIN C	10%
FAT	21 g	THIAMINE	8%
CHOLESTEROL	331 mg	RIBOFLAVIN	30%
SODIUM	390 mg	NIACIN	4%
POTASSIUM	250 mg	CALCIUM	20%
		IRON	8%

A ring of peaches brightens this skillet meal. The chutney-like glaze gives the meal a special flavor.

HAM STEAK WITH SPICED PEACH GLAZE

- **½ cup peach or apricot preserves**
- **2 tablespoons brown sugar**
- **1 teaspoon prepared mustard**
- **⅛ teaspoon ginger**
- **⅛ teaspoon cloves**
- **1 tablespoon margarine or butter**
- **1 lb. fully cooked center-cut ham slice, ½ to ¾ inch thick**
- **1 (16-oz.) can peach slices, drained**

In small bowl, combine preserves, brown sugar, mustard, ginger and cloves; blend well. Melt margarine in large skillet over medium-high heat. Add ham; cook until lightly browned on both sides. Reduce heat to low. Arrange peach slices around edge of ham slice. Spoon preserves mixture over peaches and ham. Cover; simmer 5 to 8 minutes or until thoroughly heated. 4 servings.

NUTRITION INFORMATION

SERVING SIZE: 1/4 OF RECIPE		PERCENT U.S. RDA PER SERVING	
CALORIES	350	PROTEIN	40%
PROTEIN	25 g	VITAMIN A	15%
CARBOHYDRATE	42 g	VITAMIN C	30%
FAT	9 g	THIAMINE	60%
CHOLESTEROL	60 mg	RIBOFLAVIN	15%
SODIUM	1420 mg	NIACIN	25%
POTASSIUM	500 mg	CALCIUM	2%
		IRON	15%

This microwave recipe delivers a tasty combination of south-of-the-border flavors in a flaky pie crust.

ENCHILADA-STYLE CHICKEN PIE

(pictured on right)

CRUST

1 (15-oz.) pkg. Pillsbury Refrigerated All Ready Pie Crusts
1 egg
1 teaspoon Worcestershire sauce

FILLING

1 cup chopped onions
1 (5-oz.) can chunk chicken, drained and flaked, or 1 cup cubed cooked chicken
1 (4-oz.) can chopped green chiles, well drained
¾ cup sliced ripe olives, drained
4 oz. (1 cup) shredded Monterey jack or Cheddar cheese*
½ cup milk
3 eggs
½ teaspoon salt, if desired
¼ teaspoon cumin
⅛ teaspoon garlic powder
⅛ teaspoon pepper
3 drops hot pepper sauce

TOPPINGS

Salsa, dairy sour cream, avocado slices and parsley, if desired

MICROWAVE DIRECTIONS: Prepare pie crust according to package directions for **unfilled one-crust pie** using 9-inch microwave-safe pie pan or 10-inch microwave-safe tart pan. (Refrigerate remaining crust for a later use.) Flute, if desired. Generously prick crust with fork. In medium bowl, combine 1 egg and Worcestershire sauce; blend well. Brush lightly over pie crust. (Reserve any remaining egg mixture for filling.) Microwave on HIGH for 6 to 8 minutes, rotating pan ½ turn every 2 minutes. Crust is done when surface appears dry and flaky.

Place onions in small microwave-safe bowl. Cover with microwave-safe plastic wrap. Microwave on HIGH for 3 minutes or until crisp-tender. Drain well.

To assemble pie, layer chicken, cooked onions, chiles, olives and cheese in cooked pie crust. In medium bowl, combine milk, 3 eggs, salt, cumin, garlic powder, pepper, hot pepper sauce and any remaining egg mixture; blend well. Pour mixture slowly over cheese.

Microwave on HIGH for 8 to 11 minutes or until knife inserted near center comes out clean, rotating pan once halfway through cooking. Let stand on flat surface 5 minutes before serving. Cut into wedges to serve; top each serving with salsa, sour cream, avocado slice and parsley. 6 to 8 servings.

TIP:
* A colby/Monterey jack blend cheese can be substituted for Monterey jack or Cheddar cheese.

NUTRITION INFORMATION

SERVING SIZE: 1/8 OF RECIPE		**PERCENT U.S. RDA PER SERVING**	
CALORIES	340	PROTEIN	20%
PROTEIN	14 g	VITAMIN A	35%
CARBOHYDRATE	20 g	VITAMIN C	35%
FAT	22 g	THIAMINE	4%
CHOLESTEROL	149 mg	RIBOFLAVIN	15%
SODIUM	600 mg	NIACIN	10%
POTASSIUM	330 mg	CALCIUM	20%
		IRON	10%

Garden Taco Rice

*A colorful blend of vegetables and taco seasoning gives Spanish rice a fresh new look and taste. Serve it with **Quick 'n Crunchy Cornbread Twists** (see Index) and fresh fruit.*

GARDEN TACO RICE

(our cover recipe)

- **1 lb. ground beef or ground turkey**
- **½ cup chopped onion**
- **1 (1¼-oz.) pkg. taco seasoning mix**
- **1½ cups water**
- **1½ cups thinly sliced zucchini**
- **1 cup Green Giant® Niblets® Frozen Corn (from 16-oz. pkg.)**
- **1 (14½-oz.) can stewed tomatoes**
- **1½ cups uncooked instant rice**
- **4 oz. (1 cup) shredded Cheddar cheese**

In large skillet, brown ground beef and onion; drain. Stir in remaining ingredients except rice and cheese; bring to a boil. Stir in rice. Reduce heat to low; cover and simmer 5 to 7 minutes or until liquid is absorbed, stirring occasionally. Remove from heat. Fluff mixture with fork; sprinkle with cheese. Cover; let stand 3 minutes or until cheese is melted. Garnish with cilantro and cherry tomatoes, if desired.
6 (1-cup) servings.

NUTRITION INFORMATION

SERVING SIZE: 1 CUP		PERCENT U.S. RDA PER SERVING	
CALORIES	380	PROTEIN	30%
PROTEIN	21 g	VITAMIN A	15%
CARBOHYDRATE	34 g	VITAMIN C	17%
FAT	18 g	THIAMINE	15%
CHOLESTEROL	65 mg	RIBOFLAVIN	15%
SODIUM	410 mg	NIACIN	25%
POTASSIUM	520 mg	CALCIUM	20%
		IRON	20%

Great Sauces for

These seasoned hamburger patties make a great entree. Offer the family a choice of sauces (this page) to top them off.

SAVORY BURGERS

1 lb. ground beef
¼ cup dry bread crumbs
2 tablespoons finely chopped onion
1 egg
1 teaspoon Worcestershire sauce
¼ to ½ teaspoon garlic salt
¼ teaspoon pepper

In medium bowl, combine all ingredients; mix well. Shape mixture into 4 patties. Broil or grill patties 4 to 6 inches from heat 10 to 15 minutes or until browned on both sides and no longer pink in center. Serve with desired sauce or sauces. 4 patties.

NUTRITION INFORMATION

SERVING SIZE: 1 PATTY		PERCENT U.S. RDA PER SERVING	
CALORIES	270	PROTEIN	30%
PROTEIN	21 g	VITAMIN A	*
CARBOHYDRATE	6 g	VITAMIN C	*
FAT	17 g	THIAMINE	2%
CHOLESTEROL	122 mg	RIBOFLAVIN	10%
SODIUM	370 mg	NIACIN	25%
POTASSIUM	260 mg	CALCIUM	2%
		IRON	10%

* Contains less than 2% of the U.S. RDA of this nutrient.

ITALIAN SAUCE

¾ cup prepared spaghetti sauce
¼ cup coarsely chopped ripe olives, drained

In small saucepan, combine ingredients; blend well. Cook over low heat until thoroughly heated, stirring occasionally. Serve warm. 1 cup.

NUTRITION INFORMATION

SERVING SIZE: 1 TABLESPOON		PERCENT U.S. RDA PER SERVING	
CALORIES	16	PROTEIN	*
PROTEIN	0 g	VITAMIN A	2%
CARBOHYDRATE	2 g	VITAMIN C	*
FAT	1 g	THIAMINE	*
CHOLESTEROL	0 mg	RIBOFLAVIN	*
SODIUM	75 mg	NIACIN	*
POTASSIUM	45 mg	CALCIUM	*
		IRON	*

* Contains less than 2% of the U.S. RDA of this nutrient.

CREOLE SAUCE

1 tablespoon cornstarch
2 tablespoons cold water
1 (8-oz.) can (1 cup) stewed tomatoes
¼ teaspoon garlic powder
⅛ teaspoon dried thyme leaves, crushed
⅛ teaspoon cayenne pepper, if desired
⅛ teaspoon hot pepper sauce

In small saucepan, stir cornstarch into cold water until dissolved. Add remaining ingredients; blend well. Cook and stir over low heat 3 to 4 minutes or until sauce is bubbly and slightly thickened. Serve warm. 1 cup.

NUTRITION INFORMATION

SERVING SIZE: 1 TABLESPOON		PERCENT U.S. RDA PER SERVING	
CALORIES	6	PROTEIN	*
PROTEIN	0 g	VITAMIN A	*
CARBOHYDRATE	1 g	VITAMIN C	2%
FAT	0 g	THIAMINE	*
CHOLESTEROL	0 mg	RIBOFLAVIN	*
SODIUM	35 mg	NIACIN	*
POTASSIUM	35 mg	CALCIUM	*
		IRON	*

* Contains less than 2% of the U.S. RDA of this nutrient.

Topping Burgers

BLUE CHEESE SAUCE

½ cup dairy sour cream
1 oz. (¼ cup) crumbled blue cheese

In small bowl, combine ingredients; blend well. Store in refrigerator. ½ cup.

NUTRITION INFORMATION

SERVING SIZE: 1 TABLESPOON		PERCENT U.S. RDA PER SERVING	
CALORIES	45	PROTEIN	*
PROTEIN	1 g	VITAMIN A	2%
CARBOHYDRATE	1 g	VITAMIN C	*
FAT	4 g	THIAMINE	*
CHOLESTEROL	9 mg	RIBOFLAVIN	2%
SODIUM	60 mg	NIACIN	*
POTASSIUM	30 mg	CALCIUM	2%
		IRON	*

* Contains less than 2% of the U.S. RDA of this nutrient.

MUSHROOM WINE SAUCE

2 tablespoons margarine or butter
1½ cups (4 oz.) sliced fresh mushrooms
1 tablespoon finely chopped onion
¼ cup cold water
1 tablespoon red Burgundy wine or red cooking wine
¼ teaspoon Worcestershire sauce
2 teaspoons cornstarch
Dash salt

Melt margarine in small skillet over medium heat. Add mushrooms and onion; cook and stir 2 to 3 minutes or until mushrooms are almost tender.

In small bowl, combine remaining ingredients; blend well. Stir mixture into mushrooms and onion. Cook until sauce is bubbly and thickened, stirring constantly. Serve warm. ¾ cup.

NUTRITION INFORMATION

SERVING SIZE: 1 TABLESPOON		PERCENT U.S. RDA PER SERVING	
CALORIES	20	PROTEIN	*
PROTEIN	0 g	VITAMIN A	*
CARBOHYDRATE	1 g	VITAMIN C	*
FAT	2 g	THIAMINE	*
CHOLESTEROL	0 mg	RIBOFLAVIN	2%
SODIUM	35 mg	NIACIN	*
POTASSIUM	40 mg	CALCIUM	*
		IRON	*

* Contains less than 2% of the U.S. RDA of this nutrient.

CALIFORNIA SAUCE

½ cup mayonnaise or salad dressing
1 tablespoon finely chopped onion
1 tablespoon pickle relish
4 oz. (1 cup) shredded American or Cheddar cheese
½ cup chopped seeded tomato

In medium bowl, combine all ingredients except tomato; blend well. Fold in tomato. Cover; refrigerate about 30 minutes to blend flavors. Store in refrigerator. 1½ cups.

NUTRITION INFORMATION

SERVING SIZE: 1 TABLESPOON		PERCENT U.S. RDA PER SERVING	
CALORIES	50	PROTEIN	*
PROTEIN	1 g	VITAMIN A	*
CARBOHYDRATE	1 g	VITAMIN C	*
FAT	5 g	THIAMINE	*
CHOLESTEROL	7 mg	RIBOFLAVIN	*
SODIUM	100 mg	NIACIN	*
POTASSIUM	20 mg	CALCIUM	2%
		IRON	*

* Contains less than 2% of the U.S. RDA of this nutrient.

CHEESY PEPPER SAUCE

8 oz. pasteurized process cheese food, cut into ½-inch cubes (about 2 cups)
2 tablespoons finely chopped green bell pepper
2 tablespoons finely chopped red bell pepper
1 tablespoon milk
3 drops hot pepper sauce

In small saucepan, combine all ingredients. Cook and stir over low heat until cheese is melted. Serve warm. ¾ cup.

NUTRITION INFORMATION

SERVING SIZE: 1 TABLESPOON		PERCENT U.S. RDA PER SERVING	
CALORIES	60	PROTEIN	6%
PROTEIN	4 g	VITAMIN A	4%
CARBOHYDRATE	2 g	VITAMIN C	4%
FAT	5 g	THIAMINE	*
CHOLESTEROL	12 mg	RIBOFLAVIN	4%
SODIUM	230 mg	NIACIN	*
POTASSIUM	60 mg	CALCIUM	10%
		IRON	*

* Contains less than 2% of the U.S. RDA of this nutrient.

Make-Ahead Meatballs
in Quick Meatball Stew **p. 48**

After preparing these meatballs, store them in the freezer to use in preparing ***Meatball Green Bean Stroganoff*** *(p. 47),* ***Southwest-Style Meatballs*** *(p. 46) and* ***Quick Meatball Stew*** *(p. 48). This recipe makes enough meatballs for all three variations. See our tip on how to thaw meatballs.*

MAKE-AHEAD MEATBALLS

DOUBLE USE
(pictured on left)

2 eggs
½ cup milk
2 lb. ground beef
1 cup chopped onions
¼ cup dry bread crumbs or cracker crumbs
1 teaspoon salt
¼ teaspoon pepper
1 teaspoon Worcestershire sauce

Heat oven to 400°F. In large bowl, combine eggs and milk; blend well. Stir in remaining ingredients; mix well. Shape into 36 meatballs, 1¼ to 1½ inches in diameter. Place in ungreased 15x10x1-inch pan.

Bake at 400°F. for 17 to 22 minutes or until lightly browned and thoroughly cooked. Cool 5 minutes; place meatballs in ungreased 13x9-inch pan. Freeze uncovered for 45 minutes. Place 12 partially frozen meatballs in each of 3 freezerproof containers or freezer bags; label and date.* 36 meatballs.

MICROWAVE DIRECTIONS: Prepare meatballs as directed above. Arrange half of meatballs around outer edge of 12x8-inch (2-quart) microwave-safe baking dish or on roasting rack. Cover with waxed paper. Microwave on HIGH for 5 to 9 minutes or until meatballs are thoroughly cooked, turning meatballs over and rearranging halfway through cooking. Cool 5 minutes; freeze as directed above.

TIPS:
* Meatballs can be frozen up to 3 months.

To thaw 12 meatballs, place in 2-quart microwave-safe casserole; cover. Microwave on DEFROST for 6 to 7 minutes or until thawed, rearranging meatballs once halfway through thawing. (Meatballs should be cool to the touch when thawed.) Or, thaw overnight in refrigerator.

NUTRITION INFORMATION

SERVING SIZE: 1 MEATBALL		PERCENT U.S. RDA PER SERVING	
CALORIES	60	PROTEIN	6%
PROTEIN	5 g	VITAMIN A	*
CARBOHYDRATE	1 g	VITAMIN C	*
FAT	4 g	THIAMINE	*
CHOLESTEROL	27 mg	RIBOFLAVIN	2%
SODIUM	85 mg	NIACIN	4%
POTASSIUM	65 mg	CALCIUM	*
		IRON	2%

* Contains less than 2% of the U.S. RDA of this nutrient.

Cook's Note

Freezing Foods

Freezing is an excellent method of food storage for make-ahead dishes or the remaining portion of a double-use recipe. Follow these simple steps.

1. Cool foods before freezing.

2. Wrap foods as airtight as possible using moisture and vapor-proof materials. Good choices are plastic containers with tight-fitting lids, heavy-duty plastic bags, heavy-duty foil and vacuum-sealed bags.

3. Label each package.

4. Avoid tying up a serving dish in the freezer by lining the dish with a piece of foil three times its width. Add the food to be frozen, fold down the foil edges, and press out any air. Freeze until firm. Lift out the frozen food, placing it in the freezer. When ready to serve the food, unwrap and place it back in the dish for cooking or heating.

5. Store foods at zero degrees or below.

6. Keep a list of the foods frozen.

Pinto beans are a favorite ingredient in Southwest cooking. They are plentiful in protein, vitamins, minerals, fiber and flavor and contain no cholesterol and almost no fat. Enjoy them in this satisfying main dish. Serve it over hot cooked rice or with a tossed green salad.

SOUTHWEST-STYLE MEATBALLS

(pictured on p. 48)

1 tablespoon oil
½ cup chopped onion
½ cup chopped green bell pepper
1 (15-oz.) can tomato sauce with tomato bits
1 (15-oz.) can Green Giant® or Joan of Arc® Pinto Beans or Light or Dark Red Kidney Beans, drained
2 teaspoons brown sugar
1 teaspoon chili powder
¼ teaspoon garlic powder
¼ teaspoon dried oregano leaves, crushed
¼ teaspoon cumin
12 frozen Make-Ahead Meatballs (page 45)
2 oz. (½ cup) shredded Monterey jack or Cheddar cheese

Heat oil in large skillet over medium heat. Add onion and bell pepper; cook and stir until onion is tender. Stir in remaining ingredients except cheese; bring to a boil. Reduce heat to low; cover and simmer 10 to 15 minutes or until meatballs are thoroughly heated, stirring and turning meatballs occasionally. Serve meatballs with hot cooked rice, if desired. Sprinkle with cheese.
4 to 6 servings.

MICROWAVE DIRECTIONS: Thaw meatballs as directed in tip for Make-Ahead Meatballs (page 45). **Omit oil**. In 2-quart microwave-safe casserole, combine onion and bell pepper. Cover tightly. Microwave on HIGH for 1½ to 2 minutes or until vegetables are crisp-tender. Stir in remaining ingredients except cheese; cover. Microwave on HIGH for 6 to 8 minutes or until meatballs are thoroughly heated, stirring once halfway through cooking. Serve meatballs with hot cooked rice, if desired. Sprinkle with cheese.

NUTRITION INFORMATION

SERVING SIZE: 1/6 OF RECIPE		**PERCENT U.S. RDA PER SERVING**	
CALORIES	280	PROTEIN	25%
PROTEIN	17 g	VITAMIN A	20%
CARBOHYDRATE	24 g	VITAMIN C	25%
FAT	14 g	THIAMINE	10%
CHOLESTEROL	63 mg	RIBOFLAVIN	15%
SODIUM	770 mg	NIACIN	15%
POTASSIUM	670 mg	CALCIUM	10%
		IRON	15%

Fresh green beans, so abundant in gardens and produce sections now, team up with an easy cream sauce for a delicious approach to stroganoff.

MEATBALL GREEN BEAN STROGANOFF

(pictured on p. 49)

1 tablespoon oil
2 cups fresh green beans, broken into 2-inch pieces*
1/3 cup red bell pepper strips, 1 inch long
1/3 cup chopped onion
1 garlic clove, minced, or 1/2 teaspoon chopped garlic in oil
1 (10 1/2-oz.) can condensed cream of chicken soup
1/4 cup water
1 tablespoon Worcestershire sauce
12 frozen Make-Ahead Meatballs (page 45)
1 cup dairy sour cream
Hot cooked noodles or mashed potatoes

Heat oil in large skillet over medium heat. Add green beans, bell pepper, onion and garlic; cook and stir 4 to 6 minutes or until onion is crisp-tender. Stir in soup, water, Worcestershire sauce and frozen meatballs; bring to a boil. Reduce heat to low; cover and simmer 15 minutes or until meatballs are thoroughly heated and green beans are tender, stirring and turning meatballs occasionally.

Stir in sour cream; heat over low heat until warm, stirring occasionally. To serve, spoon stroganoff mixture over noodles. 4 to 6 servings.

MICROWAVE DIRECTIONS:
Thaw meatballs as directed in tip for Make-Ahead Meatballs (page 45). **Omit oil**. In 2-quart microwave-safe casserole, combine 1/4 cup water, green beans, red pepper, onion and garlic; cover. Microwave on HIGH for 6 to 7 minutes or until green beans are warm and almost crisp-tender, stirring once halfway through cooking. Stir in soup, Worcestershire sauce and meatballs; cover. Microwave on HIGH for 5 to 6 minutes or until meatballs are thoroughly heated and green beans are tender, stirring once halfway through cooking.

Stir in sour cream; cover. Microwave on HIGH for 2 to 3 minutes or until thoroughly heated. Stir before serving. To serve, spoon stroganoff mixture over noodles.

TIP:
* Two cups Green Giant® Frozen Cut Green Beans (from 16-oz. pkg.) can be substituted for fresh green beans.

NUTRITION INFORMATION

SERVING SIZE: 1/6 OF RECIPE		**PERCENT U.S. RDA PER SERVING**	
CALORIES	510	PROTEIN	30%
PROTEIN	20 g	VITAMIN A	25%
CARBOHYDRATE	52 g	VITAMIN C	20%
FAT	24 g	THIAMINE	25%
CHOLESTEROL	129 mg	RIBOFLAVIN	20%
SODIUM	630 mg	NIACIN	25%
POTASSIUM	370 mg	CALCIUM	10%
		IRON	25%

To create meals in minutes, your pantry should contain canned soups and frozen or canned vegetables. In this recipe, these ingredients are combined with ***Make-Ahead Meatballs*** *(p. 45) for a flavorful stew ready in 20 minutes.*

QUICK MEATBALL STEW

(pictured on right)

1 (10½-oz.) can condensed beef broth
1⅓ cups water
1 (16-oz.) pkg. Green Giant® American Mixtures™ New England Style Frozen Peas, Potatoes and Carrots
12 frozen Make-Ahead Meatballs (page 45)
1 medium onion, cut into 1-inch pieces
1 teaspoon dried basil leaves, crushed
⅛ teaspoon pepper
¼ cup flour
¼ cup cold water

In 4-quart saucepan or Dutch oven, combine all ingredients except flour and ¼ cup water; bring to a boil. Reduce heat to low; cover and simmer 10 minutes or until meatballs are thoroughly heated and vegetables are tender, stirring occasionally.

In small jar with tight-fitting lid, combine flour and ¼ cup water; shake well. Gradually stir into stew mixture; cook until thickened, stirring frequently. Serve in individual bowls. 4 (1¼-cup) servings.

NUTRITION INFORMATION

SERVING SIZE: 1-1/4 CUPS		PERCENT U.S. RDA PER SERVING	
CALORIES	330	PROTEIN	35%
PROTEIN	22 g	VITAMIN A	100%
CARBOHYDRATE	30 g	VITAMIN C	20%
FAT	15 g	THIAMINE	20%
CHOLESTEROL	81 mg	RIBOFLAVIN	15%
SODIUM	740 mg	NIACIN	30%
POTASSIUM	610 mg	CALCIUM	6%
		IRON	20%

Pictured clockwise from top: Quick Meatball Stew, Meatball Green Bean Stroganoff p. 47, Southwest-Style Meatballs p. 46

SIDE DISHES & SALADS

Sensational yet simple, these dishes will dress-up any dinner.

To solve your no-time-for-making-dinner dilemma use convenient, quality take-out. You'll save meal-making minutes by shopping the deli and salad bar. For example, buy already-prepared cole slaw mix for **Fresh Fruit and Slaw** or "personalize" deli potato salad with sliced radishes and cucumber, sour cream and dill. Other creative "homemade" solutions include:

- **Creamy Dill Pasta (using refrigerated pasta)**
- **Walnut Chicken Salad (using deli salad)**
- **Basil Vegetable Pasta Salad with Beef (using deli meat)**

Pictured clockwise from top: ***Easy Cheesy Pasta p. 52, Saucy Swiss Pasta p. 53, Creamy Dill Pasta p. 52***

Our instant no-cook dill sauce melts over the hot pasta in this recipe to make an incredibly easy side dish.

CREAMY DILL PASTA

(pictured on p. 50)

7 to 9 oz. uncooked mostaccioli, rotini or medium shells

DILL SAUCE

½ cup dairy sour cream
2 tablespoons milk
1 teaspoon onion salt
1 teaspoon dried dill weed
⅛ teaspoon pepper

In unsalted water, cook pasta to desired doneness as directed on package. Drain; rinse with hot water. Meanwhile, in small bowl combine all sauce ingredients; blend well. Pour over hot pasta; toss to coat. 8 (½-cup) servings.

NUTRITION INFORMATION

SERVING SIZE: 1/2 CUP		PERCENT U.S. RDA PER SERVING	
CALORIES	130	PROTEIN	6%
PROTEIN	4 g	VITAMIN A	2%
CARBOHYDRATE	18 g	VITAMIN C	*
FAT	4 g	THIAMINE	15%
CHOLESTEROL	30 mg	RIBOFLAVIN	10%
SODIUM	220 mg	NIACIN	4%
POTASSIUM	90 mg	CALCIUM	2%
		IRON	6%

* Contains less than 2% of the U.S. RDA of this nutrient.

This well-flavored cheese sauce is so easy to make it could replace the convenience pasta mixes in your pantry.

EASY CHEESY PASTA

(pictured on p. 50)

7 to 9 oz. uncooked radiatore, wagon wheel pasta or elbow macaroni

CHEESE SAUCE

¼ cup milk
4 oz. (1 cup) cubed American cheese
2 teaspoons prepared mustard
¼ teaspoon salt
Dash pepper
2 tablespoons chopped pimiento, drained

In unsalted water, cook pasta to desired doneness as directed on package. Drain; rinse with hot water. Meanwhile, in small saucepan combine all sauce ingredients except pimiento. Cook and stir over low heat until cheese is melted. Stir in pimiento. Pour over hot pasta; toss to coat. 6 (½-cup) servings.

MICROWAVE DIRECTIONS: Cook pasta as directed above. In 2-cup microwave-safe measuring cup, combine all sauce ingredients except pimiento. Microwave on HIGH for 1½ to 2 minutes, stirring once halfway through cooking. Stir again until mixture is smooth. Stir in pimiento. Pour over hot pasta; toss to coat.

NUTRITION INFORMATION

SERVING SIZE: 1/2 CUP		PERCENT U.S. RDA PER SERVING	
CALORIES	200	PROTEIN	15%
PROTEIN	9 g	VITAMIN A	6%
CARBOHYDRATE	24 g	VITAMIN C	2%
FAT	7 g	THIAMINE	20%
CHOLESTEROL	50 mg	RIBOFLAVIN	15%
SODIUM	390 mg	NIACIN	6%
POTASSIUM	125 mg	CALCIUM	15%
		IRON	8%

Any of our sauced pasta side dishes can become a quick main dish by adding about a cup of cubed cooked meat and a cup of cooked vegetables.

SAUCY SWISS PASTA

(pictured on p. 51)

7 to 9 oz. uncooked linguine, fettuccine or spaghetti

SWISS SAUCE

1½ cups milk
2 tablespoons flour
1 tablespoon Dijon mustard
½ teaspoon salt
3 oz. (¾ cup) shredded Swiss cheese
1 tablespoon chopped fresh parsley or 1 teaspoon dried parsley flakes

In unsalted water, cook pasta to desired doneness as directed on package. Drain; rinse with hot water. Meanwhile, in small saucepan using wire whisk, blend milk, flour, mustard and salt until smooth. Stir in cheese. Cook over medium heat 5 minutes or until sauce is bubbly and thickened, stirring frequently. Stir in parsley. Pour over hot pasta; toss to coat. 6 (½-cup) servings.

MICROWAVE DIRECTIONS: Cook pasta as directed above. In 4-cup microwave-safe measuring cup using wire whisk, blend milk, flour, mustard and salt until smooth. Microwave on HIGH for 4 to 5 minutes or until mixture thickens and boils, stirring twice during cooking. Stir in cheese and parsley, stirring until cheese is melted. Pour over hot pasta; toss to coat.

NUTRITION INFORMATION

SERVING SIZE: 1/2 CUP		PERCENT U.S. RDA PER SERVING	
CALORIES	220	PROTEIN	15%
PROTEIN	11 g	VITAMIN A	6%
CARBOHYDRATE	29 g	VITAMIN C	*
FAT	6 g	THIAMINE	25%
CHOLESTEROL	49 mg	RIBOFLAVIN	20%
SODIUM	330 mg	NIACIN	8%
POTASSIUM	190 mg	CALCIUM	20%
		IRON	8%

* Contains less than 2% of the U.S. RDA of this nutrient.

Cook's Note

Making Rice and Pasta Ahead

Rice and pasta can be cooked ahead and frozen in single-serving, family or recipe-sized portions to eliminate this cooking step during dinner preparation. Cook rice or pasta to the doneness you wish and cool it completely before packaging it for freezing.

To freeze single servings, place ½-cup portions of cooked rice or pasta in 6-ounce custard cups. Cover and freeze until firm. Remove the frozen portions from the custard cups. Place them in freezerproof containers; label and date. **For family or recipe-sized portions**, freeze cooked rice or pasta in 2-cup portions in freezerproof containers.

To reheat single servings, return the frozen rice or pasta to custard cups. *Do not add water*. Cover with waxed paper. Microwave on HIGH until thoroughly heated, allowing 1 to 1½ minutes per serving.

To reheat family or recipe-sized portions, place a 2-cup portion of frozen rice or pasta in a microwave-safe bowl. *Add 2 tablespoons of water*. Cover with waxed paper. Microwave on HIGH 5 minutes or until thoroughly heated, stirring once halfway through cooking.

The fresh flavors of cucumber and dill give purchased potato salad a homemade taste.

DRESSED-UP DELI POTATO SALAD

(pictured on right)

1 lb. (about 2 cups) prepared potato salad
½ cup coarsely chopped peeled cucumber
⅓ cup sliced radishes
⅓ cup dairy sour cream
½ teaspoon dried dill weed

In large bowl, combine all ingredients; blend well. Serve in lettuce-lined bowl, if desired. 5 (½-cup) servings.

NUTRITION INFORMATION

SERVING SIZE: 1/2 CUP		PERCENT U.S. RDA PER SERVING	
CALORIES	170	PROTEIN	4%
PROTEIN	3 g	VITAMIN A	6%
CARBOHYDRATE	12 g	VITAMIN C	12%
FAT	11 g	THIAMINE	4%
CHOLESTEROL	69 mg	RIBOFLAVIN	4%
SODIUM	490 mg	NIACIN	4%
POTASSIUM	300 mg	CALCIUM	4%
		IRON	4%

Dressed-Up Deli Potato Salad

Tender, deep green spinach leaves make a delicious salad. When eaten raw, they are a good source of vitamins A and C. Look for cleaned spinach leaves packed for your convenience in the produce section of your supermarket.

LIGHT AND LEMONY SPINACH SALAD

LEMON DRESSING

¼ cup oil
2 tablespoons lemon juice
1 tablespoon chopped fresh parsley or 1 teaspoon dried parsley flakes
1 teaspoon sugar
¼ teaspoon salt
⅛ teaspoon pepper
2 green onions, sliced

SALAD

4 cups cleaned fresh spinach, torn into bite-sized pieces
2 tablespoons shelled sunflower seeds

In small jar with tight-fitting lid, combine all dressing ingredients; shake well. Place spinach in large bowl. Pour dressing over spinach; toss lightly to coat. Sprinkle with sunflower seeds. 4 servings.

NUTRITION INFORMATION

SERVING SIZE: 1/4 OF RECIPE		PERCENT U.S. RDA PER SERVING	
CALORIES	160	PROTEIN	4%
PROTEIN	3 g	VITAMIN A	80%
CARBOHYDRATE	5 g	VITAMIN C	35%
FAT	16 g	THIAMINE	2%
CHOLESTEROL	0 mg	RIBOFLAVIN	6%
SODIUM	170 mg	NIACIN	4%
POTASSIUM	380 mg	CALCIUM	6%
		IRON	10%

Young dandelion greens add a tart, slightly bitter taste to salads. If you choose to pick the dandelion greens, pick those free of chemicals and wash them thoroughly.

GREENS WITH MUSTARD VINAIGRETTE

4 cups assorted salad greens (spinach leaves, escarole, chicory or dandelion greens)
1 ripe tomato, peeled, chopped

DRESSING

¼ cup olive oil or oil
2 tablespoons red wine vinegar
1 tablespoon Dijon mustard

In large bowl, combine salad greens and tomato; toss lightly. In small jar with tight-fitting lid, combine all dressing ingredients; shake well. Pour dressing over salad mixture; toss lightly to coat. Serve immediately. 4 servings.

NUTRITION INFORMATION

SERVING SIZE: 1/4 OF RECIPE		PERCENT U.S. RDA PER SERVING	
CALORIES	140	PROTEIN	2%
PROTEIN	1 g	VITAMIN A	50%
CARBOHYDRATE	3 g	VITAMIN C	25%
FAT	14 g	THIAMINE	2%
CHOLESTEROL	0 mg	RIBOFLAVIN	4%
SODIUM	140 mg	NIACIN	2%
POTASSIUM	310 mg	CALCIUM	4%
		IRON	6%

Cook's Note

Salad On-Hand

A tossed salad can round out many meals. To get a salad on the table fast, keep a mixture of torn salad greens on hand in the refrigerator. Store the cleaned and torn greens in a sealed plastic bag or covered plastic container with a paper towel in the bottom of the container to absorb any excess water. Prepared greens can be stored up to three days.

In this new approach to preparing fresh spinach, the leaves are first wilted, then quickly stir-fried in a lightly sweetened browned butter. This quick cooking method retains the fresh color and flavor of the spinach.

SO-GOOD SPINACH

2 tablespoons butter or margarine
½ teaspoon sugar
8 cups cleaned fresh spinach
1 quart boiling water

In large skillet, combine butter and sugar. Cook over low heat until sugar is dissolved and butter is light golden brown, stirring occasionally.

Place spinach in large colander or strainer. Pour boiling water over spinach. Add spinach to butter mixture; cook and stir 2 to 3 minutes or until thoroughly heated. Serve immediately. 4 (½-cup) servings.

NUTRITION INFORMATION

SERVING SIZE: 1/2 CUP		PERCENT U.S. RDA PER SERVING	
CALORIES	80	PROTEIN	4%
PROTEIN	3 g	VITAMIN A	150%
CARBOHYDRATE	4 g	VITAMIN C	35%
FAT	6 g	THIAMINE	6%
CHOLESTEROL	16 mg	RIBOFLAVIN	10%
SODIUM	150 mg	NIACIN	4%
POTASSIUM	630 mg	CALCIUM	10%
		IRON	15%

The delicate flavor of dill accents the natural sweetness of the peas.

DILLED SWEET PEAS

2 cups Green Giant® Frozen Sweet Peas (from 16-oz. pkg.)
¼ cup finely chopped onion
2 tablespoons chopped pimiento, drained
1 tablespoon margarine or butter
¼ to ½ teaspoon dried dill weed
¼ teaspoon salt

Cook peas with onion until crisp-tender as directed on package; drain. Stir in remaining ingredients; cook until thoroughly heated.
4 (½-cup) servings.

NUTRITION INFORMATION

SERVING SIZE: 1/2 CUP		PERCENT U.S. RDA PER SERVING	
CALORIES	80	PROTEIN	6%
PROTEIN	4 g	VITAMIN A	15%
CARBOHYDRATE	11 g	VITAMIN C	25%
FAT	3 g	THIAMINE	10%
CHOLESTEROL	0 mg	RIBOFLAVIN	4%
SODIUM	240 mg	NIACIN	6%
POTASSIUM	135 mg	CALCIUM	2%
		IRON	6%

Cook's Note

Herbs

Herbs add flavor and variety to meals and are especially important when cooking times are short and flavors have less time to develop. To get the full flavor of herbs, follow these guidelines:

• Store herbs in tightly covered containers in a dark place.

• Do not freeze herbs or store them near hot appliances.

• When using a dried herb, measure it first, then crush the leaves between your fingers to release the flavor and aroma. If the aroma is weak, the flavor will be weak, and the herb should be replaced.

• For full flavor in recipes that cook quickly, add herbs at the beginning of cooking time. In many recipes, we have given a range in measurement to accommodate individual taste preferences.

• To substitute a fresh herb for a dried herb, use three times the amount called for.

• To substitute a ground dried herb for dried leaves, use half the amount called for.

Cook's Note

Crisp-Tender Doneness

"Crisp-tender" is a term used in our recipes to describe vegetables that are cooked but not soft or mushy. They are slightly firm when bitten and bright in color. Vegetables cooked to a crisp-tender doneness retain nutrition and add quality to hot mixtures like casseroles or to cold mixtures like salads.

A unique combination of vegetables and fruit is blended with thyme and a light sauce flavored with apple juice.

HARVEST TIME GREEN BEANS

(pictured above)

½ lb. fresh green beans, broken into 2-inch pieces (2 cups)*
1 cup thinly sliced carrots
2 green onions, cut into ½-inch pieces
½ cup water
1 teaspoon sugar
¼ teaspoon dried thyme leaves, crushed
¼ teaspoon salt
1 teaspoon cornstarch
⅓ cup apple juice
½ cup cubed unpeeled red apple

Harvest Time Green Beans

In large saucepan, combine green beans, carrots, green onions, water, sugar, thyme and salt; bring to a boil. Reduce heat to low; cover and simmer 5 to 7 minutes or until vegetables are crisp-tender, stirring occasionally.

In small bowl, stir cornstarch into apple juice until dissolved. Gradually stir cornstarch mixture into cooked vegetables; add apple. Cook and stir 1 to 2 minutes or until sauce is bubbly and thickened and apple is warm. 6 (½-cup) servings.

MICROWAVE DIRECTIONS:
In 2-quart microwave-safe casserole, combine green beans, carrots, green onions, ¼ cup water, sugar, thyme and salt. Cover tightly. Microwave on HIGH for 7 to 8 minutes or until green beans are almost tender, stirring once halfway through cooking.

In small bowl, stir cornstarch into apple juice until dissolved. Gradually stir cornstarch mixture into cooked vegetables. Microwave uncovered on HIGH for 2 minutes; stir in apple. Microwave on HIGH 2 to 3 minutes or until sauce is thickened and vegetables are crisp-tender, stirring once halfway through cooking.

TIP:
* Two cups Green Giant® Frozen Cut Green Beans (from 16-oz. pkg.) can be substituted for fresh green beans.

NUTRITION INFORMATION

SERVING SIZE: 1/2 CUP		PERCENT U.S. RDA PER SERVING	
CALORIES	35	PROTEIN	*
PROTEIN	1 g	VITAMIN A	120%
CARBOHYDRATE	9 g	VITAMIN C	10%
FAT	0 g	THIAMINE	2%
CHOLESTEROL	0 mg	RIBOFLAVIN	2%
SODIUM	95 mg	NIACIN	2%
POTASSIUM	170 mg	CALCIUM	2%
		IRON	2%

* Contains less than 2% of the U.S. RDA of this nutrient.

Green Chile 'n Cheese Biscuit Bread

This nacho-flavored, pull-apart dinner bread is fun to serve with soups or chowders.

GREEN CHILE 'N CHEESE BISCUIT BREAD

(pictured above)

- **1 (10-oz.) can Hungry Jack® Refrigerated Flaky Biscuits**
- **1 tablespoon margarine or butter, melted**
- **¼ teaspoon chili powder**
- **3 tablespoons chopped seeded fresh or canned green chiles, drained**
- **2 oz. (½ cup) shredded colby/ Monterey jack blend cheese or colby cheese**

Heat oven to 400°F. Lightly grease cookie sheet. Separate dough into 10 biscuits. Place 1 biscuit in center of greased cookie sheet. Arrange remaining biscuits in circle, edges slightly overlapping, around center biscuit. Gently press out to 10-inch circle.

In small bowl, combine margarine and chili powder; brush over biscuits. Sprinkle with chiles and cheese. Bake at 400°F. for 10 to 17 minutes or until deep golden brown. To serve, pull apart warm biscuits. 10 servings.

NUTRITION INFORMATION

SERVING SIZE: 1/10 OF RECIPE		PERCENT U.S. RDA PER SERVING	
CALORIES	120	PROTEIN	4%
PROTEIN	3 g	VITAMIN A	6%
CARBOHYDRATE	12 g	VITAMIN C	6%
FAT	7 g	THIAMINE	6%
CHOLESTEROL	5 mg	RIBOFLAVIN	4%
SODIUM	340 mg	NIACIN	4%
POTASSIUM	30 mg	CALCIUM	4%
		IRON	4%

What a great idea to utilize the natural triangular shape and rich flaky texture of refrigerated crescent dough to create these flavorful wedges of garlic toast.

CRESCENT GARLIC TOAST

(pictured on p. 63)

1 (8-oz.) can Pillsbury Refrigerated Quick Crescent Dinner Rolls
3 tablespoons prepared Caesar salad dressing
3 tablespoons grated Parmesan cheese
¼ teaspoon dried basil leaves, crushed

Heat oven to 375°F. Separate dough into 8 triangles. Place on ungreased cookie sheet. Generously brush each triangle with salad dressing. In small bowl, combine Parmesan cheese and basil. Sprinkle over each triangle. Bake at 375°F. for 8 to 11 minutes or until golden brown. 8 servings.

NUTRITION INFORMATION

SERVING SIZE: 1/8 OF RECIPE		PERCENT U.S. RDA PER SERVING	
CALORIES	140	PROTEIN	4%
PROTEIN	3 g	VITAMIN A	*
CARBOHYDRATE	11 g	VITAMIN C	*
FAT	9 g	THIAMINE	4%
CHOLESTEROL	5 mg	RIBOFLAVIN	4%
SODIUM	350 mg	NIACIN	4%
POTASSIUM	70 mg	CALCIUM	4%
		IRON	4%

* Contains less than 2% of the U.S. RDA of this nutrient.

*For flavor variety, sprinkle half the dough with sesame or poppy seeds and half with chopped walnuts. Serve this simple bread with **Quick and Easy Chili** (see Index).*

QUICK 'N CRUNCHY CORNBREAD TWISTS

(pictured on p. 78)

1 (11.5-oz.) can Pillsbury Refrigerated Cornbread Twists
1 tablespoon margarine or butter, melted
2 tablespoons sesame seed, poppy seed or finely chopped walnuts

Heat oven to 375°F. Unroll dough. Brush with margarine. Sprinkle with sesame seed; press lightly into dough. Separate at perforations into 16 strips. Twist each strip and place on 1 large or 2 small ungreased cookie sheets, pressing ends down firmly. Bake at 375°F. for 10 to 15 minutes or until light golden brown. 16 servings.

NUTRITION INFORMATION

SERVING SIZE: 1/16 OF RECIPE		PERCENT U.S. RDA PER SERVING	
CALORIES	80	PROTEIN	2%
PROTEIN	2 g	VITAMIN A	*
CARBOHYDRATE	9 g	VITAMIN C	*
FAT	5 g	THIAMINE	4%
CHOLESTEROL	0 mg	RIBOFLAVIN	2%
SODIUM	160 mg	NIACIN	2%
POTASSIUM	20 mg	CALCIUM	*
		IRON	2%

* Contains less than 2% of the U.S. RDA of this nutrient.

GARDEN VEGETABLE MACARONI SALAD

DOUBLE USE

DRESSING

¾ cup prepared ranch salad dressing
½ teaspoon Dijon mustard
¼ teaspoon salt
⅛ teaspoon pepper

SALAD

4½ oz. (1 cup) uncooked elbow macaroni
1 (16-oz.) pkg. Green Giant® American Mixtures™ Heartland Style Frozen Broccoli, Cauliflower and Carrots
½ cup sliced radishes
2 tablespoons finely chopped onion

In small bowl, combine all dressing ingredients; blend well. Set aside. Cook macaroni to desired doneness as directed on package. Drain; rinse with cold water. Meanwhile, cook vegetables until crisp-tender as directed on package. Drain; rinse with cold water.

In large bowl, combine all salad ingredients; toss lightly. Pour dressing over salad mixture; toss lightly to coat. Cover; refrigerate about 30 minutes to blend flavors. 11 (½-cup) servings.

NUTRITION INFORMATION

SERVING SIZE: 1/2 CUP		**PERCENT U.S. RDA PER SERVING**	
CALORIES	90	PROTEIN	2%
PROTEIN	2 g	VITAMIN A	20%
CARBOHYDRATE	9 g	VITAMIN C	20%
FAT	6 g	THIAMINE	6%
CHOLESTEROL	0 mg	RIBOFLAVIN	4%
SODIUM	190 mg	NIACIN	4%
POTASSIUM	125 mg	CALCIUM	*
		IRON	2%

* Contains less than 2% of the U.S. RDA of this nutrient.

VARIATION: VEGETABLE MACARONI SALAD WITH HAM
When combining salad ingredients, add 1 to 1½ cups cubed cooked ham.

BASIL VEGETABLE PASTA SALAD

BASIL DRESSING

3 tablespoons olive oil or oil
3 tablespoons white wine vinegar
2 tablespoons finely chopped fresh basil or 1 tablespoon dried basil leaves, crushed
½ teaspoon salt
¼ teaspoon garlic powder
⅛ teaspoon pepper

SALAD

4 oz. (1 cup) uncooked mostaccioli (tube-shaped macaroni)
1 (16-oz.) pkg. Green Giant® American Mixtures™ San Francisco Style Frozen Broccoli, Carrots, Water Chestnuts and Red Peppers
1 (2¼-oz.) can (¼ cup) sliced ripe olives, drained

In small bowl using wire whisk, blend all dressing ingredients. Set aside. Cook mostaccioli to desired doneness as directed on package. Drain; rinse with cold water. Meanwhile, cook vegetables until crisp-tender as directed on package. Drain; rinse with cold water.

In large bowl, combine all salad ingredients; toss lightly. Pour dressing over salad mixture; toss lightly to coat. Cover; refrigerate about 30 minutes to blend flavors. 5 (1-cup) servings.

NUTRITION INFORMATION

SERVING SIZE: 1 CUP		**PERCENT U.S. RDA PER SERVING**	
CALORIES	200	PROTEIN	6%
PROTEIN	5 g	VITAMIN A	45%
CARBOHYDRATE	25 g	VITAMIN C	35%
FAT	10 g	THIAMINE	20%
CHOLESTEROL	0 mg	RIBOFLAVIN	6%
SODIUM	360 mg	NIACIN	10%
POTASSIUM	270 mg	CALCIUM	6%
		IRON	10%

VARIATION: VEGETABLE PASTA SALAD WITH BEEF (pictured on right)
When combining salad ingredients, add 4 to 6 oz. thinly sliced cooked roast beef, cut into 2x½-inch strips.

Crescent Garlic Toast p. 61, Vegetable Pasta Salad with Beef

"Refreshing" was the word used by our taste panel members to describe this colorful salad, which was inspired by Thai cuisine.

CUCUMBER TOMATO THAI SALAD

SALAD

1 medium cucumber, peeled
1 medium tomato, cut into 8 wedges
2 green onions, cut into ½-inch pieces
2 to 4 tablespoons chopped fresh cilantro

DRESSING

1 tablespoon sugar
3 tablespoons lime juice
1 tablespoon soy sauce
Dash cayenne pepper, if desired

Cut cucumber into 8 lengthwise spears; cut each spear crosswise into ½-inch slices. Cut tomato wedges in half crosswise. In large bowl, combine all salad ingredients; toss lightly. In small bowl, combine all dressing ingredients; blend well. Pour over salad mixture; toss lightly to coat. Cover; refrigerate about 30 minutes to blend flavors. 6 (½-cup) servings.

NUTRITION INFORMATION

SERVING SIZE: 1/2 CUP		PERCENT U.S. RDA PER SERVING	
CALORIES	25	PROTEIN	*
PROTEIN	1 g	VITAMIN A	6%
CARBOHYDRATE	6 g	VITAMIN C	15%
FAT	0 g	THIAMINE	*
CHOLESTEROL	0 mg	RIBOFLAVIN	*
SODIUM	180 mg	NIACIN	*
POTASSIUM	140 mg	CALCIUM	*
		IRON	2%

* Contains less than 2% of the U.S. RDA of this nutrient.

To simplify the preparation of this recipe, use a food processor to slice the carrots and to chop the onion.

HERBED CARROTS AND GRAPES

2 tablespoons margarine or butter
3 cups thinly sliced carrots
½ cup finely chopped onion
3 tablespoons dry sherry or water
¾ to 1 cup red or green seedless grapes, halved
Dash dried thyme leaves or dill weed
1 tablespoon honey

Melt margarine in medium skillet. Add carrots, onion and sherry. Cover; cook over medium-high heat 3 to 5 minutes or until carrots are crisp-tender, stirring occasionally. Remove from heat; stir in remaining ingredients. Cover; let stand 1 to 2 minutes until grapes are warm. 6 (½-cup) servings.

NUTRITION INFORMATION

SERVING SIZE: 1/2 CUP		PERCENT U.S. RDA PER SERVING	
CALORIES	110	PROTEIN	*
PROTEIN	1 g	VITAMIN A	350%
CARBOHYDRATE	16 g	VITAMIN C	10%
FAT	4 g	THIAMINE	6%
CHOLESTEROL	0 mg	RIBOFLAVIN	2%
SODIUM	65 mg	NIACIN	2%
POTASSIUM	280 mg	CALCIUM	2%
		IRON	2%

* Contains less than 2% of the U.S. RDA of this nutrient.

When purchasing corn on the cob, select ears with plump kernels, fresh green husks and brightly colored silk.

CORN ON THE COB WITH LEMON CHIVE BUTTER

4 quarts cold water
1 tablespoon sugar, if desired
8 ears corn, husked, cleaned

LEMON CHIVE BUTTER
½ cup butter or margarine, softened
1 to 2 tablespoons chopped fresh chives or 1 to 2 teaspoons freeze-dried chives
1 teaspoon grated lemon peel

In 5-quart saucepan or Dutch oven, bring water and sugar to a boil; add corn. Reduce heat to low; cover and simmer 5 to 8 minutes or until kernels are tender. Remove corn from water. Meanwhile, in small bowl combine all butter ingredients. Brush ears with butter mixture. Serve with remaining butter. 8 servings.

MICROWAVE DIRECTIONS:
In 12x8-inch (2-quart) microwave-safe baking dish, place 4 ears of the corn, alternating wide and narrow ends in dish. **Add ¼ cup water**. Cover with microwave-safe plastic wrap. Microwave on HIGH for 12 to 14 minutes or until kernels are tender, turning dish ½ turn halfway through cooking. Repeat with remaining 4 ears of corn. Prepare butter and serve as directed above.

NUTRITION INFORMATION

SERVING SIZE: 1/8 OF RECIPE		**PERCENT U.S. RDA PER SERVING**	
CALORIES	180	PROTEIN	4%
PROTEIN	3 g	VITAMIN A	15%
CARBOHYDRATE	17 g	VITAMIN C	8%
FAT	13 g	THIAMINE	10%
CHOLESTEROL	31 mg	RIBOFLAVIN	2%
SODIUM	130 mg	NIACIN	8%
POTASSIUM	250 mg	CALCIUM	*
		IRON	2%

* Contains less than 2% of the U.S. RDA of this nutrient.

Summer squash and tomatoes are among late summer's bounty of vegetables. They are enhanced in this recipe with the flavor of basil and Parmesan cheese.

SUMMER HARVEST BOUNTY

1 tablespoon margarine or butter
2 cups thinly sliced zucchini
2 cups thinly sliced yellow squash
½ cup coarsely chopped onion
½ teaspoon dried basil leaves, crushed
¼ teaspoon garlic salt
1 medium tomato, cubed
⅓ cup freshly grated Parmesan cheese or 3 tablespoons grated Parmesan cheese

Melt margarine in large skillet over medium-high heat. Add zucchini, squash and onion; cook and stir 3 minutes. Sprinkle with basil and garlic salt; cook and stir an additional 3 to 5 minutes or until vegetables are crisp-tender. Stir in tomato; cook 1 minute or until tomato is thoroughly heated. Sprinkle with Parmesan cheese. 8 (½-cup) servings.

NUTRITION INFORMATION

SERVING SIZE: 1/2 CUP		**PERCENT U.S. RDA PER SERVING**	
CALORIES	50	PROTEIN	4%
PROTEIN	3 g	VITAMIN A	6%
CARBOHYDRATE	4 g	VITAMIN C	10%
FAT	3 g	THIAMINE	4%
CHOLESTEROL	3 mg	RIBOFLAVIN	2%
SODIUM	150 mg	NIACIN	2%
POTASSIUM	200 mg	CALCIUM	6%
		IRON	2%

A variation of classic nicoise salad, this main dish salad is special enough for company.

SALMON SALAD WITH PEARS

CREAMY PARSLEY HONEY DRESSING

- **¾ cup mayonnaise or salad dressing**
- **¼ cup honey**
- **2 tablespoons buttermilk or plain yogurt**
- **2 tablespoons chopped fresh parsley or 1 teaspoon dried parsley flakes**
- **1 teaspoon dry mustard**
- **¼ teaspoon lemon juice**

SALAD

- **1 (9-oz.) pkg. Green Giant® Harvest Fresh® Frozen Baby Lima Beans**
- **2 cups sliced zucchini**
- **2 medium pears or apples, sliced (about 2 cups)**
- **1 (16-oz.) can salmon, drained, flaked**
- **Spinach or lettuce leaves**

In small bowl using wire whisk, blend all dressing ingredients. Cover; refrigerate.

Cook lima beans as directed on package. Drain; rinse with cold water. Arrange lima beans, zucchini, pears and salmon on each of 4 to 6 spinach-lined plates. Spoon dressing over salads; garnish as desired.
4 to 6 servings.

NUTRITION INFORMATION

SERVING SIZE: 1/6 OF RECIPE		PERCENT U.S. RDA PER SERVING	
CALORIES	360	PROTEIN	25%
PROTEIN	17 g	VITAMIN A	30%
CARBOHYDRATE	32 g	VITAMIN C	15%
FAT	20 g	THIAMINE	6%
CHOLESTEROL	38 mg	RIBOFLAVIN	10%
SODIUM	540 mg	NIACIN	20%
POTASSIUM	700 mg	CALCIUM	20%
		IRON	10%

When melon is unavailable, tomato wedges can be used in this salad. Or, serve the chicken mixture on sourdough bread slices as an open-faced sandwich and garnish it with tomato slices.

WALNUT CHICKEN SALAD

- **1 lb. (2 cups) prepared chicken salad**
- **⅓ cup chopped walnuts, toasted***
- **1 teaspoon Dijon mustard**
- **½ teaspoon dried tarragon leaves, crushed**
- **1 small cantaloupe or honeydew melon, cut into quarters lengthwise, seeds and rind removed**
- **Spinach or lettuce leaves**
- **Toasted walnut halves, if desired**

In medium bowl, combine chicken salad, chopped walnuts, mustard and tarragon; mix well. Cut each cantaloupe quarter lengthwise into 4 slices. Arrange 4 slices on each of 4 spinach-lined plates. Spoon ½ cup chicken mixture onto each plate next to cantaloupe slices. Garnish with walnut halves. 4 servings.

TIP:
* To toast walnuts, spread nuts on cookie sheet; bake at 350°F. for 5 to 7 minutes or until golden brown, stirring occasionally. Or, spread nuts in thin layer in microwave-safe pie pan. Microwave on HIGH for 4 to 5 minutes or until golden brown, stirring frequently.

NUTRITION INFORMATION

SERVING SIZE: 1/4 OF RECIPE		PERCENT U.S. RDA PER SERVING	
CALORIES	400	PROTEIN	40%
PROTEIN	26 g	VITAMIN A	70%
CARBOHYDRATE	12 g	VITAMIN C	50%
FAT	28 g	THIAMINE	10%
CHOLESTEROL	126 mg	RIBOFLAVIN	15%
SODIUM	510 mg	NIACIN	35%
POTASSIUM	640 mg	CALCIUM	6%
		IRON	10%

Apple Pear Salad

When starting dinner, prepare this refreshing cinnamon fruit salad first and then refrigerate it until serving time.

APPLE PEAR SALAD

(pictured above)

SALAD

- **1 cup cubed unpeeled red apple**
- **1 cup cubed unpeeled pear**
- **1 cup red or green seedless grapes, halved**
- **1 teaspoon lemon juice**

DRESSING

- **¼ cup mayonnaise or salad dressing**
- **2 tablespoons honey**
- **⅛ teaspoon cinnamon**

In medium bowl, combine all salad ingredients except lemon juice. Sprinkle with lemon juice; toss lightly. In small bowl, combine all dressing ingredients; blend well. Pour over salad mixture; toss lightly to coat. Serve in lettuce-lined bowl, if desired. 5 (½-cup) servings.

NUTRITION INFORMATION

SERVING SIZE: 1/2 CUP		**PERCENT U.S. RDA PER SERVING**	
CALORIES	160	PROTEIN	*
PROTEIN	1 g	VITAMIN A	*
CARBOHYDRATE	21 g	VITAMIN C	10%
FAT	9 g	THIAMINE	2%
CHOLESTEROL	6 mg	RIBOFLAVIN	2%
SODIUM	65 mg	NIACIN	*
POTASSIUM	130 mg	CALCIUM	*
		IRON	*

* Contains less than 2% of the U.S. RDA of this nutrient.

These baked potatoes can be easily added to your quick dinner menus.

QUICK BAKED POTATOES

4 small baking potatoes
¼ teaspoon onion salt
¼ teaspoon garlic salt
¼ cup margarine or butter
Paprika

Heat oven to 425°F. Cut potatoes in half lengthwise. With tip of knife, score cut side of each half in crisscross pattern. Sprinkle potatoes lightly with salts; dot with margarine. Place in ungreased shallow baking pan. Bake at 425°F. for about 30 minutes or until tender. Sprinkle with paprika. 4 servings.

MICROWAVE DIRECTIONS:
Prepare potatoes as directed above. Place in 8-inch (2-quart) microwave-safe baking dish. Cover. Microwave on HIGH for 10 to 12 minutes or until potatoes begin to feel tender. Remove from oven; let stand covered 5 minutes. Sprinkle with paprika.

NUTRITION INFORMATION

SERVING SIZE: 1/4 OF RECIPE		PERCENT U.S. RDA PER SERVING	
CALORIES	270	PROTEIN	6%
PROTEIN	4 g	VITAMIN A	8%
CARBOHYDRATE	38 g	VITAMIN C	25%
FAT	12 g	THIAMINE	10%
CHOLESTEROL	0 mg	RIBOFLAVIN	2%
SODIUM	360 mg	NIACIN	10%
POTASSIUM	640 mg	CALCIUM	*
		IRON	10%

* Contains less than 2% of the U.S. RDA of this nutrient.

Serve this cheesy potato accompaniment with a broiled steak and spinach salad.

POTATOES ROMANOFF

2 cups frozen hash browns, thawed*
1 teaspoon instant minced onion
¼ teaspoon salt
⅛ teaspoon garlic powder
⅔ cup cottage cheese
⅓ cup dairy sour cream
2 oz. (½ cup) shredded Cheddar cheese
Paprika

Heat oven to 350°F. Grease 1-quart casserole. In medium bowl, combine all ingredients except ¼ cup of the Cheddar cheese and paprika; mix well. Spoon into greased casserole. Bake at 350°F. for 25 to 30 minutes or until thoroughly heated. Sprinkle with remaining cheese and paprika during last 5 minutes of baking time. 6 (½-cup) servings.

MICROWAVE DIRECTIONS:
To thaw hash browns, microwave on DEFROST for 8 to 10 minutes, breaking up hash browns and rearranging halfway through cooking. Grease 1-quart microwave-safe casserole. In medium bowl, combine all ingredients except ¼ cup of the Cheddar cheese and paprika; mix well. Spoon into greased casserole. Microwave on HIGH for 6 to 8 minutes. Sprinkle with remaining cheese and paprika. Microwave on HIGH for 1 to 2 minutes or until cheese begins to melt.

TIP:
* Two cups diced cooked potatoes can be substituted for the hash browns.

NUTRITION INFORMATION

SERVING SIZE: 1/2 CUP		PERCENT U.S. RDA PER SERVING	
CALORIES	130	PROTEIN	10%
PROTEIN	7 g	VITAMIN A	2%
CARBOHYDRATE	14 g	VITAMIN C	6%
FAT	5 g	THIAMINE	4%
CHOLESTEROL	14 mg	RIBOFLAVIN	6%
SODIUM	260 mg	NIACIN	6%
POTASSIUM	240 mg	CALCIUM	10%
		IRON	4%

Brown rice is wonderful because of its nutty flavor. Now that instant brown rice is available, it fits nicely into quick meal plans.

SOUTHWEST BROWN RICE PILAF

- **1 tablespoon oil**
- **½ cup chopped onion**
- **1 garlic clove, minced, or ½ teaspoon chopped garlic in oil**
- **1 cup chicken broth**
- **1 cup uncooked instant whole grain brown rice**
- **1 (11-oz.) can Green Giant® Mexicorn® Whole Kernel Golden Sweet Corn with Red and Green Sweet Peppers, drained**
- **½ teaspoon chili powder**
- **¼ teaspoon dried oregano leaves, crushed**

Heat oil in large saucepan over medium heat. Add onion and garlic; cook and stir until onion is tender. Add broth; bring to a boil. Stir in remaining ingredients. Reduce heat to low; cover and simmer 7 to 10 minutes or until liquid is absorbed. Remove from heat. Salt to taste, if desired. Before serving, fluff with fork. 6 (½-cup) servings.

NUTRITION INFORMATION

SERVING SIZE: 1/2 CUP		PERCENT U.S. RDA PER SERVING	
CALORIES	130	PROTEIN	6%
PROTEIN	4 g	VITAMIN A	2%
CARBOHYDRATE	23 g	VITAMIN C	6%
FAT	4 g	THIAMINE	4%
CHOLESTEROL	0 mg	RIBOFLAVIN	2%
SODIUM	270 mg	NIACIN	10%
POTASSIUM	200 mg	CALCIUM	*
		IRON	4%

* Contains less than 2% of the U.S. RDA of this nutrient.

Couscous is a granular pasta originating in North Africa. It cooks in just five minutes to serve as a quick side dish.

PARSLEY BUTTERED COUSCOUS

- **1 teaspoon chicken-flavor instant bouillon**
- **1½ cups water**
- **2 teaspoons margarine or butter**
- **1 cup uncooked couscous**
- **¼ cup chopped fresh parsley or 1 tablespoon dried parsley flakes**

In medium saucepan, combine bouillon, water and margarine. Bring to a boil; remove from heat. Stir in couscous and parsley. Cover; let stand 5 minutes. Before serving, fluff with fork. 6 (½-cup) servings.

MICROWAVE DIRECTIONS:
In 4-cup microwave-safe measuring cup or 1-quart casserole, combine bouillon, water and margarine. Microwave on HIGH for 4 to 4½ minutes or until mixture comes to a boil. Stir in couscous and parsley. Cover; let stand 5 minutes. Before serving, fluff with fork.

NUTRITION INFORMATION

SERVING SIZE: 1/2 CUP		PERCENT U.S. RDA PER SERVING	
CALORIES	130	PROTEIN	6%
PROTEIN	4 g	VITAMIN A	2%
CARBOHYDRATE	24 g	VITAMIN C	2%
FAT	2 g	THIAMINE	2%
CHOLESTEROL	0 mg	RIBOFLAVIN	*
SODIUM	80 mg	NIACIN	4%
POTASSIUM	65 mg	CALCIUM	*
		IRON	2%

* Contains less than 2% of the U.S. RDA of this nutrient.

For a fast approach to preparing this salad, purchase cleaned, cut-up cauliflower and broccoli in the produce section or salad bar of your supermarket. Serve this salad with grilled or broiled meat for a quick dinner.

SUNNY CAULIFLOWER BROCCOLI TOSS

(pictured on left)

DRESSING

- **½ cup mayonnaise or salad dressing**
- **2 tablespoons sugar**
- **1 tablespoon cider vinegar**

SALAD

- **2 cups cauliflower florets**
- **2 cups cut-up fresh broccoli (including tender part of stalks)**
- **½ cup raisins**
- **¼ cup sliced green onions**
- **¼ cup shelled sunflower seeds**
- **3 slices bacon, crisply cooked, crumbled**

In small bowl using wire whisk, blend all dressing ingredients. In large bowl, combine all salad ingredients; toss lightly. Pour dressing over salad mixture; toss lightly to coat. Sprinkle with additional sunflower seeds, if desired. 8 (½-cup) servings.

NUTRITION INFORMATION

SERVING SIZE: 1/2 CUP		PERCENT U.S. RDA PER SERVING	
CALORIES	190	PROTEIN	4%
PROTEIN	3 g	VITAMIN A	8%
CARBOHYDRATE	14 g	VITAMIN C	70%
FAT	14 g	THIAMINE	4%
CHOLESTEROL	10 mg	RIBOFLAVIN	2%
SODIUM	160 mg	NIACIN	4%
POTASSIUM	290 mg	CALCIUM	2%
		IRON	4%

Skillet Barbecued Pork Chops p. 31, Sunny California Broccoli Toss

Here's a perked-up version of pear and cottage cheese salad. Add a drop or two of almond extract to the jam for added flavor.

PEAR RASPBERRY COTTAGE CHEESE SALAD

2 ripe medium pears
Lettuce leaves
Lemon juice
1 cup cottage cheese
1/3 cup seedless red raspberry jam or red currant jelly
Fresh raspberries or red seedless grapes, if desired

Cut each pear in half; remove core. Slice each pear half into 4 slices. Arrange 4 slices on each of 4 lettuce-lined plates. Brush cut surfaces of pear slices with lemon juice. Spoon 1/4 cup cottage cheese onto each plate next to pear slices.

Melt jam in small saucepan over low heat, stirring constantly. Spoon over cottage cheese and pear slices. Garnish with raspberries. 4 servings.

TIP:
To melt jam in microwave, place in small microwave-safe bowl. Microwave on HIGH for 10 to 15 seconds or until jam is melted; stir.

NUTRITION INFORMATION

SERVING SIZE: 1/4 OF RECIPE		PERCENT U.S. RDA PER SERVING	
CALORIES	150	PROTEIN	10%
PROTEIN	8 g	VITAMIN A	*
CARBOHYDRATE	27 g	VITAMIN C	8%
FAT	1 g	THIAMINE	*
CHOLESTEROL	5 mg	RIBOFLAVIN	8%
SODIUM	230 mg	NIACIN	*
POTASSIUM	160 mg	CALCIUM	4%
		IRON	2%

* Contains less than 2% of the U.S. RDA of this nutrient.

Because it takes time to shred cabbage and carrots, coleslaw is often eliminated from quick meal planning. Put it back among your menu choices by using prepared slaw mix, available in the supermarket produce section.

FRESH FRUIT AND SLAW

DRESSING
1/2 cup salad dressing or mayonnaise
1/4 cup vanilla or peach yogurt

SALAD
1/2 cup halved green or red seedless grapes
1/2 cup cubed nectarine or peeled peach
1/2 cup cubed unpeeled red apple
1 to 2 teaspoons lemon juice
4 cups prepared coleslaw mix
1 tablespoon chopped peanuts or shelled sunflower seeds, if desired

In small bowl, combine dressing ingredients; blend well. In large bowl, combine all salad ingredients except peanuts; toss lightly. Pour dressing over salad mixture; toss lightly to coat. Cover; refrigerate about 30 minutes to blend flavors. Sprinkle with peanuts.
8 (1/2-cup) servings.

NUTRITION INFORMATION

SERVING SIZE: 1/2 CUP		PERCENT U.S. RDA PER SERVING	
CALORIES	90	PROTEIN	2%
PROTEIN	1 g	VITAMIN A	2%
CARBOHYDRATE	10 g	VITAMIN C	30%
FAT	6 g	THIAMINE	2%
CHOLESTEROL	4 mg	RIBOFLAVIN	2%
SODIUM	125 mg	NIACIN	*
POTASSIUM	160 mg	CALCIUM	2%
		IRON	*

* Contains less than 2% of the U.S. RDA of this nutrient.

This tangy lemon honey dressing complements many fresh fruits. Why not double the dressing to have it on hand to use with other fruit combinations?

SUMMER FRUIT COMBO

LEMONADE HONEY DRESSING

2 tablespoons oil
2 tablespoons honey
2 tablespoons frozen lemonade concentrate, thawed
¼ teaspoon poppy seed
Dash salt

SALAD

1 cup halved red seedless grapes
1 cup watermelon cubes
1 medium nectarine, sliced
1 medium pear, sliced

In small jar with tight-fitting lid, combine all dressing ingredients; shake well. In medium bowl, combine all salad ingredients. Pour dressing over salad mixture; toss lightly to coat. Cover; refrigerate about 30 minutes to blend flavors. 8 (½-cup) servings.

NUTRITION INFORMATION

SERVING SIZE: 1/2 CUP		PERCENT U.S. RDA PER SERVING	
CALORIES	100	PROTEIN	*
PROTEIN	1 g	VITAMIN A	4%
CARBOHYDRATE	17 g	VITAMIN C	8%
FAT	4 g	THIAMINE	2%
CHOLESTEROL	0 mg	RIBOFLAVIN	2%
SODIUM	20 mg	NIACIN	*
POTASSIUM	130 mg	CALCIUM	*
		IRON	*

* Contains less than 2% of the U.S. RDA of this nutrient.

Here's a tasty stuffing you can prepare quickly with purchased seasoned bread cubes.

SAUCEPAN STUFFING

¼ cup margarine or butter
¼ cup shredded carrot
¼ cup chopped celery
¼ cup chopped onion
1 cup water
4 cups whole wheat and white seasoned bread cubes

Melt margarine in large saucepan over medium heat. Add carrot, celery and onion; cook and stir until vegetables are tender. Add water; bring to a boil. Remove from heat. Add bread cubes; toss lightly to combine. Cover; let stand 5 to 10 minutes or until liquid is absorbed. Salt and pepper to taste, if desired. Before serving, fluff with fork. 8 (½-cup) servings.

MICROWAVE DIRECTIONS: Place margarine in 2-quart microwave-safe casserole. Microwave on HIGH for 45 to 60 seconds or until melted. Stir in carrot, celery and onion. Microwave on HIGH for 1½ to 2 minutes or until vegetables are tender. Add water and bread cubes; toss lightly to combine. Cover tightly. Microwave on HIGH for 5 to 6 minutes or until liquid is absorbed and stuffing is hot, stirring once halfway through cooking. Salt and pepper to taste, if desired. Before serving, fluff with fork.

NUTRITION INFORMATION

SERVING SIZE: 1/2 CUP		PERCENT U.S. RDA PER SERVING	
CALORIES	110	PROTEIN	2%
PROTEIN	2 g	VITAMIN A	25%
CARBOHYDRATE	12 g	VITAMIN C	*
FAT	6 g	THIAMINE	2%
CHOLESTEROL	1 mg	RIBOFLAVIN	2%
SODIUM	270 mg	NIACIN	2%
POTASSIUM	60 mg	CALCIUM	2%
		IRON	2%

* Contains less than 2% of the U.S. RDA of this nutrient.

Serving simple foods attractively enhances "meal appeal."

Easy, out-of-the-ordinary touches add a full-meal flair to soups and sandwiches:

- **Crescent Garlic Toast** will enhance the ethnic flavor of **Tortellini Spinach Soup.**
- Colorful paper plates with bright napkins make **Zucchini Corn Scramble Pita** more fun to eat.
- **Quick 'n Crunchy Cornbread Twists** pair perfectly with **Cheesy Tuna Vegetable Chowder.**

Pictured top to bottom: ***Tortellini Spinach Soup p 76, Oriental Vegetable Noodle Soup p. 76***

Adding your choice of cut-up vegetables and meats makes this soup a heartier version of the popular oriental noodle soup mix.

ORIENTAL VEGETABLE NOODLE SOUP

(pictured on p. 74)

2 cups chicken or beef broth
2 cups water
½ cup Green Giant® Frozen Broccoli Cuts, Sweet Peas or Niblets® Corn (from 16-oz. pkg.)
½ cup julienne-sliced carrots
½ cup thin diagonally sliced celery
1 (3-oz.) pkg. any flavor oriental noodle soup mix
1½ cups cut-up cooked chicken, turkey, roast beef, ham or shrimp
3 tablespoons sliced green onions

In large saucepan, combine broth and water; bring to a boil. Add frozen vegetables, carrots and celery; cook 1 minute. Partially break up noodles from soup mix; stir into boiling broth. Reduce heat to low; simmer 3 minutes or until vegetables are crisp-tender. Stir in seasoning from packet in soup mix and meat; simmer an additional 2 to 3 minutes or until thoroughly heated. Garnish each serving with green onions.
3 (1½-cup) servings.

NUTRITION INFORMATION

SERVING SIZE: 1-1/2 CUPS		PERCENT U.S. RDA PER SERVING	
CALORIES	310	PROTEIN	45%
PROTEIN	28 g	VITAMIN A	130%
CARBOHYDRATE	23 g	VITAMIN C	20%
FAT	11 g	THIAMINE	15%
CHOLESTEROL	62 mg	RIBOFLAVIN	15%
SODIUM	1100 mg	NIACIN	50%
POTASSIUM	500 mg	CALCIUM	4%
		IRON	10%

The appealing appearance and flavor of this pasta soup makes it a perfect choice when unexpected company is coming for dinner. Serve it with ***Crescent Garlic Toast*** *(see Index).*

TORTELLINI SPINACH SOUP

(pictured on p. 74)

1 tablespoon olive oil or oil
1 cup thinly sliced carrots
½ cup chopped onion
1 garlic clove, minced, or ½ teaspoon chopped garlic in oil
3 (14½-oz.) cans chicken broth
1 (9-oz. pkg.) refrigerated uncooked cheese-filled tortellini
2 cups Green Giant® Frozen Cut Leaf Spinach (from 16-oz. pkg.)
½ teaspoon dried oregano leaves, crushed
2 oz. (½ cup) shredded mozzarella cheese

Heat oil in 4-quart saucepan or Dutch oven over medium heat. Add carrots, onion and garlic; cook and stir until onion is tender. Add broth; bring to a boil. Add tortellini; boil gently 4 to 5 minutes or until tortellini is almost tender. Add spinach and oregano; simmer 2 to 3 minutes or until spinach is tender, stirring occasionally. Sprinkle each serving with cheese. 6 (1-cup) servings.

NUTRITION INFORMATION

SERVING SIZE: 1 CUP		PERCENT U.S. RDA PER SERVING	
CALORIES	230	PROTEIN	25%
PROTEIN	15 g	VITAMIN A	200%
CARBOHYDRATE	27 g	VITAMIN C	20%
FAT	7 g	THIAMINE	20%
CHOLESTEROL	29 mg	RIBOFLAVIN	20%
SODIUM	940 mg	NIACIN	25%
POTASSIUM	530 mg	CALCIUM	25%
		IRON	15%

This quick version of German bean soup has great flavor, color and texture. Serve it with crusty bread and wedges of apple.

QUICK TWO BEAN SOUP

¼ cup margarine or butter
⅔ cup thinly sliced carrots
¼ cup chopped onion
2 (11½-oz.) cans condensed bean with bacon soup
2⅔ cups water
1 cup Green Giant® Frozen Cut Green Beans (from 16-oz. pkg.)
¼ teaspoon dried oregano leaves, crushed

Melt margarine in large saucepan over medium heat. Add carrots and onion; cook and stir until onion is tender. Stir in remaining ingredients; bring to a boil. Reduce heat to low; cover and simmer 10 to 15 minutes or until vegetables are crisp-tender, stirring occasionally.
6 (1 cup) servings.

NUTRITION INFORMATION

SERVING SIZE: 1 CUP		PERCENT U.S. RDA PER SERVING	
CALORIES	200	PROTEIN	10%
PROTEIN	7 g	VITAMIN A	100%
CARBOHYDRATE	25 g	VITAMIN C	4%
FAT	11 g	THIAMINE	6%
CHOLESTEROL	3 mg	RIBOFLAVIN	2%
SODIUM	900 mg	NIACIN	4%
POTASSIUM	410 mg	CALCIUM	8%
		IRON	10%

A versatile pantry item for quick meals is canned soups. They are a source of inspiration for casseroles, pasta sauces and satisfying chowders, as in this recipe.

QUICK CORN CHOWDER

2 cups Green Giant® Niblets® Frozen Corn (from 16-oz. pkg.)
1 (10¾-oz.) can condensed cream of potato soup
1 cup milk
2 tablespoons chopped pimiento, drained, if desired
⅛ teaspoon pepper
4 slices bacon, crisply cooked, crumbled

In medium saucepan, cook corn until crisp-tender as directed on package; drain. Stir in remaining ingredients; cook until thoroughly heated, stirring occasionally. 3 (1-cup) servings.

NUTRITION INFORMATION

SERVING SIZE: 1 CUP		PERCENT U.S. RDA PER SERVING	
CALORIES	250	PROTEIN	15%
PROTEIN	10 g	VITAMIN A	15%
CARBOHYDRATE	36 g	VITAMIN C	25%
FAT	8 g	THIAMINE	15%
CHOLESTEROL	18 mg	RIBOFLAVIN	15%
SODIUM	990 mg	NIACIN	15%
POTASSIUM	520 mg	CALCIUM	10%
		IRON	6%

Grilled cheese sandwiches make a great accompaniment for this satisfying vegetable soup.

HEARTY TOMATO BEAN SOUP

(pictured on right)

- **2 slices bacon**
- **½ cup chopped onion**
- **½ cup chopped celery**
- **1 (28-oz.) can whole tomatoes, cut up**
- **1 (10¾-oz.) can condensed tomato soup**
- **1 (15.5-oz.) can Green Giant® or Joan of Arc® Light or Dark Red Kidney Beans, drained**
- **1 (11-oz.) can Green Giant® Niblets® Whole Kernel Sweet Corn, undrained**
- **½ cup water**
- **1 teaspoon sugar**
- **¼ teaspoon dried thyme leaves, crushed**
- **⅛ teaspoon pepper**

Cook bacon in 4-quart saucepan or Dutch oven until crisp; remove bacon, reserving 1 tablespoon drippings. Crumble bacon; set aside. Heat reserved drippings in saucepan over medium heat. Add onion and celery; cook and stir until vegetables are crisp-tender. Stir in remaining ingredients; bring to a boil. Reduce heat to low; cover and simmer 10 to 15 minutes or until thoroughly heated. Garnish each serving with crumbled bacon.
6 (1⅓-cup) servings.

NUTRITION INFORMATION

SERVING SIZE: 1-1/3 CUPS		PERCENT U.S. RDA PER SERVING	
CALORIES	170	PROTEIN	10%
PROTEIN	8 g	VITAMIN A	25%
CARBOHYDRATE	34 g	VITAMIN C	60%
FAT	3 g	THIAMINE	10%
CHOLESTEROL	2 mg	RIBOFLAVIN	6%
SODIUM	840 mg	NIACIN	10%
POTASSIUM	660 mg	CALCIUM	8%
		IRON	15%

Hearty Tomato Bean Soup, Quick 'n Crunchy Cornbread Twists p. 61

Swiss cheese adds a subtle new flavor to tuna salad sandwiches. Apples and celery provide great color and texture.

GRILLED TUNA AND SWISS

1 (6½-oz.) can tuna, drained, flaked
4 oz. (1 cup) shredded Swiss cheese
½ cup chopped celery
½ cup finely chopped unpeeled red apple
¼ cup mayonnaise or salad dressing
¼ cup plain yogurt
1 tablespoon finely chopped fresh parsley or 1 teaspoon dried parsley flakes
10 slices Vienna bread
Margarine or butter

In medium bowl, combine all ingredients except bread and margarine; mix well. To assemble sandwiches, spread ½ cup of tuna mixture on each of 5 slices of bread. Cover with remaining bread slices. Spread margarine on outside of each sandwich.

Heat large skillet over medium-high heat or heat griddle to 375°F. Add sandwiches; cook 1 to 2 minutes on each side or until bread browns and sandwiches are hot. 5 sandwiches.

NUTRITION INFORMATION

SERVING SIZE: 1 SANDWICH		PERCENT U.S. RDA PER SERVING	
CALORIES	430	PROTEIN	30%
PROTEIN	21 g	VITAMIN A	10%
CARBOHYDRATE	31 g	VITAMIN C	2%
FAT	25 g	THIAMINE	15%
CHOLESTEROL	35 mg	RIBOFLAVIN	15%
SODIUM	600 mg	NIACIN	30%
POTASSIUM	260 mg	CALCIUM	30%
		IRON	15%

A meal in a roll! Serve these filled kaiser rolls with ***Apple Pear Salad*** *(see Index) for an easy meal.*

BROCCOLI HAM AND SWISS ROLLS

2 tablespoons margarine or butter
2 tablespoons flour
½ cup milk
1 (9-oz.) pkg. Green Giant® Frozen Cut Broccoli, thawed, drained
¼ cup dairy sour cream
1 teaspoon lemon juice
¼ teaspoon hot pepper sauce
4 (4-inch) kaiser rolls, unsliced
4 thin slices cooked ham
4 slices tomato, ¼ inch thick
4 thin slices Swiss cheese

Melt margarine in medium saucepan over low heat. Stir in flour; cook and stir until mixture is smooth and bubbly. Gradually stir in milk. Cook over medium heat until mixture thickens and boils, stirring constantly. Add broccoli, sour cream, lemon juice and hot pepper sauce. Cook until thoroughly heated, stirring occasionally.

Using sharp knife, remove ½-inch slice from top of each roll; set aside. Remove bread from inside of rolls, leaving about ½-inch shell. Spoon about ⅓ cup of hot broccoli mixture into each roll. Place on ungreased cookie sheet or broiler pan. Top each with 1 slice ham, 1 slice tomato and 1 slice cheese. Broil 4 to 6 inches from heat 1 to 2 minutes or until cheese is melted. Place top of roll on each sandwich. 4 sandwiches.

NUTRITION INFORMATION

SERVING SIZE: 1 SANDWICH		PERCENT U.S. RDA PER SERVING	
CALORIES	410	PROTEIN	30%
PROTEIN	20 g	VITAMIN A	40%
CARBOHYDRATE	40 g	VITAMIN C	50%
FAT	20 g	THIAMINE	25%
CHOLESTEROL	44 mg	RIBOFLAVIN	25%
SODIUM	660 mg	NIACIN	15%
POTASSIUM	360 mg	CALCIUM	40%
		IRON	10%

A great-tasting meal in a bun.

SALAD AND SANDWICH ROLLS

4 (6-inch) French or hero sandwich rolls
8 to 10 oz. thinly sliced deli meats (corned beef, roast beef, pork, ham, chicken and/or turkey)
4 oz. thinly sliced deli cheeses (Swiss, Cheddar, American, Monterey jack, muenster and/or pepper cheese)
Spinach or leaf lettuce
8 thin slices tomato
8 thin slices cucumber
4 thin slices onion, separated into rings, if desired
Favorite creamy salad dressing

Cut sandwich rolls in half lengthwise. Place cut side up on ungreased cookie sheet or broiler pan. On bottom half of each roll, layer ¼ of the meat and cheese slices. Broil 4 to 6 inches from heat 1 to 2 minutes or until cheese is melted and top halves of rolls are toasted. Layer ¼ of the spinach, tomato, cucumber and onion over cheese on each bottom half; drizzle with salad dressing. Top each sandwich with toasted top of roll. 4 sandwiches.

MICROWAVE DIRECTIONS: Cut sandwich rolls in half lengthwise. On bottom half of each roll, layer ¼ of the meat and cheese slices; place each on microwave-safe plate. Microwave each on HIGH for 1 to 2 minutes or until cheese is melted. If desired, microwave each top of roll on HIGH for 10 to 15 seconds or until warm. Continue as directed above.

NUTRITION INFORMATION

SERVING SIZE: 1 SANDWICH		PERCENT U.S. RDA PER SERVING	
CALORIES	570	PROTEIN	45%
PROTEIN	29 g	VITAMIN A	30%
CARBOHYDRATE	48 g	VITAMIN C	25%
FAT	29 g	THIAMINE	25%
CHOLESTEROL	98 mg	RIBOFLAVIN	25%
SODIUM	1440 mg	NIACIN	25%
POTASSIUM	390 mg	CALCIUM	35%
		IRON	25%

A fork and knife will be needed to eat this hearty open-faced sandwich.

HOT BRAT 'N TATER SANDWICHES

3 precooked bratwurst, cut into ½-inch slices
1 medium onion, sliced
1 (15.5-oz.) can German potato salad
4 to 5 slices dark rye bread
4 to 5 (4x4-inch) slices Swiss cheese
Chopped fresh parsley, if desired

In large skillet over medium heat, cook and stir bratwurst and onion until onion is tender. Drain, if desired. Stir in potato salad. Cook over low heat about 3 minutes or until potato salad is thoroughly heated, stirring occasionally.

To assemble sandwiches, place bread slices on ungreased cookie sheet or broiler pan. Spoon bratwurst mixture evenly over each slice; top each with cheese slice. Broil 4 to 6 inches from heat 2 to 3 minutes or until cheese is melted.* Garnish each with parsley. 5 sandwiches.

TIP:
* To melt cheese in microwave, place 1 to 2 sandwiches on microwave-safe plate. Microwave on HIGH for 1 to 2 minutes or until cheese is melted. Repeat with remaining sandwiches.

NUTRITION INFORMATION

SERVING SIZE: 1 SANDWICH		PERCENT U.S. RDA PER SERVING	
CALORIES	420	PROTEIN	30%
PROTEIN	19 g	VITAMIN A	6%
CARBOHYDRATE	35 g	VITAMIN C	2%
FAT	23 g	THIAMINE	25%
CHOLESTEROL	54 mg	RIBOFLAVIN	15%
SODIUM	1020 mg	NIACIN	15%
POTASSIUM	380 mg	CALCIUM	30%
		IRON	10%

Gyros Sandwiches

Gyros are Greek pocket sandwiches filled with strips of cooked lamb and slices of onion and tomato, then drizzled with a zesty yogurt dressing. Our recipe combines ground beef and ground lamb for an easy burger version.

GYROS SANDWICHES

(pictured above)

DRESSING

1 cup plain yogurt
1 tablespoon lemon juice
¼ teaspoon salt
¼ teaspoon dried dill weed
1 garlic clove, minced, or ½ teaspoon chopped garlic in oil

SANDWICHES

½ lb. ground lamb
½ lb. ground beef
½ teaspoon salt
¼ teaspoon allspice
1 garlic clove, minced, or ½ teaspoon chopped garlic in oil
2 (6 to 7-inch) pocket breads
Shredded lettuce
1 medium onion, thinly sliced
1 medium tomato, thinly sliced

In small bowl, combine all dressing ingredients; blend well. Set aside. In large bowl, combine lamb, beef, salt, allspice and garlic; mix well. Shape mixture into 4 patties. In large skillet over medium heat, cook patties 3 to

4 minutes on each side or until browned on both sides and no longer pink in center. Warm pocket breads as directed on package.

To assemble sandwiches, cut each warm pocket bread in half crosswise, forming 2 pockets. Place shredded lettuce in bottom of each pocket. Layer meat patty and onion and tomato slices in each; drizzle with dressing. 4 sandwiches.

NUTRITION INFORMATION

SERVING SIZE: 1 SANDWICH		PERCENT U.S. RDA PER SERVING	
CALORIES	380	PROTEIN	40%
PROTEIN	25 g	VITAMIN A	6%
CARBOHYDRATE	29 g	VITAMIN C	15%
FAT	17 g	THIAMINE	20%
CHOLESTEROL	71 mg	RIBOFLAVIN	25%
SODIUM	710 mg	NIACIN	30%
POTASSIUM	560 mg	CALCIUM	15%
		IRON	15%

A scrambled egg sandwich with a new twist—cheesy vegetable-laden eggs are stuffed inside whole wheat pocket breads!

ZUCCHINI CORN SCRAMBLE PITA

- **1 to 2 tablespoons margarine or butter**
- **½ cup Green Giant® Niblets® Frozen Corn (from 16-oz. pkg.)**
- **½ cup thinly sliced zucchini**
- **¼ cup chopped onion**
- **¼ cup chopped red or green bell pepper**
- **¼ teaspoon garlic salt**
- **¼ teaspoon dried oregano leaves, crushed**
- **6 eggs**
- **⅓ cup milk**
- **2 oz. (½ cup) cubed Swiss cheese**
- **3 (6 to 7-inch) whole wheat pocket breads**
- **Lettuce leaves, if desired**

Melt margarine in large skillet over medium heat. Add frozen corn, zucchini, onion and bell pepper; cook and stir 5 minutes or until vegetables are crisp-tender. Sprinkle with garlic salt and oregano.

In medium bowl, combine eggs and milk; blend well. Pour over vegetable mixture; reduce heat to low. Cook until eggs are almost set but still moist, stirring occasionally from outside edge to center, allowing uncooked egg to flow to bottom of skillet. Fold in cheese; cook until cheese is softened. Warm pocket breads as directed on package.

To assemble sandwiches, cut each warm pocket bread in half crosswise forming 2 pockets. Stuff each pocket with lettuce and egg mixture. 6 sandwiches.

MICROWAVE DIRECTIONS: Place **1 tablespoon margarine** in 1½ to 2-quart microwave-safe casserole. Microwave on HIGH for 30 to 40 seconds or until melted. Stir in frozen corn, zucchini, onion and bell pepper. Microwave on HIGH for 1½ to 2 minutes or until vegetables are crisp-tender, stirring once halfway through cooking. Sprinkle with garlic salt and oregano.

In medium bowl, combine eggs and milk; blend well. Pour over vegetable mixture; stir to combine. Microwave on HIGH for 4½ to 5 minutes or until eggs are almost set but still moist, stirring cooked egg mixture to center of casserole halfway through cooking. Fold in cheese. Cover tightly. Let stand 2 to 3 minutes or until cheese has softened. Assemble sandwiches as directed above.

NUTRITION INFORMATION

SERVING SIZE: 1 SANDWICH		PERCENT U.S. RDA PER SERVING	
CALORIES	270	PROTEIN	25%
PROTEIN	15 g	VITAMIN A	20%
CARBOHYDRATE	24 g	VITAMIN C	10%
FAT	12 g	THIAMINE	10%
CHOLESTEROL	222 mg	RIBOFLAVIN	25%
SODIUM	220 mg	NIACIN	10%
POTASSIUM	180 mg	CALCIUM	15%
		IRON	10%

Cook's Note

Turkey

Fresh turkey cuts, now readily available in many supermarkets, are great for quick meals because they cook in a short period of time. In this cookbook, the fresh turkey products used in recipes include turkey breast tenderloins and slices and ground turkey. Other products you may find available include turkey breast steaks and portions, sausage and bacon.

A **turkey breast tenderloin** is the meat cut lengthwise from the breast bone. It is an elongated, thick cut that looks somewhat like a fish fillet. A **turkey breast slice** is cut crosswise from the tenderloin. It looks like a boneless pork chop. **Ground turkey** is made from different cuts of turkey and has a pink color and smooth texture.

Fresh turkey cuts should be stored in the coldest part of the refrigerator (up to two days). For longer storage (up to six months), wrap the turkey in freezerproof paper containers, label, date and freeze.

When you crave an old-fashioned turkey dinner but don't have the time to prepare it, try these sandwiches. They contain all the flavors of that special meal.

TURKEY DINNER SANDWICHES

1 egg
1 tablespoon water
½ cup dry bread crumbs
½ teaspoon onion salt or garlic salt
¼ teaspoon poultry seasoning
5 fresh turkey breast slices
1 to 2 tablespoons margarine or butter
1 cup prepared turkey gravy or 1 (.87-oz.) pkg. turkey gravy mix
5 (¾ inch thick) slices multi-grain or French bread
⅔ to 1 cup whole berry cranberry sauce

In shallow dish, combine egg and water; blend well. In another shallow dish, combine bread crumbs, onion salt and poultry seasoning; blend well. Dip turkey slices in egg mixture; coat with bread crumb mixture.

Melt margarine in large skillet over medium heat. Add turkey slices; cook 2 to 3 minutes on each side or until golden brown; keep warm. In small saucepan, heat or prepare gravy as directed on package.

To assemble sandwiches, spread each slice of bread with 2 to 3 tablespoons of the cranberry sauce; place on plates. Top each with warm turkey slice; spoon 2 to 3 tablespoons gravy over each sandwich. Pass any remaining gravy. 5 sandwiches.

NUTRITION INFORMATION

SERVING SIZE: 1 SANDWICH		PERCENT U.S. RDA PER SERVING	
CALORIES	390	PROTEIN	50%
PROTEIN	31 g	VITAMIN A	4%
CARBOHYDRATE	46 g	VITAMIN C	*
FAT	9 g	THIAMINE	10%
CHOLESTEROL	114 mg	RIBOFLAVIN	20%
SODIUM	780 mg	NIACIN	40%
POTASSIUM	360 mg	CALCIUM	4%
		IRON	15%

* Contains less than 2% of the U.S. RDA of this nutrient.

Serve these tasty sandwiches with tomato soup, crunchy vegetable sticks and a glass of milk.

EGGS 'N HAM BISCUIT SANDWICHES

- **1 (12-oz.) can Big Country® Refrigerated Buttermilk Biscuits**
- **1 tablespoon margarine or butter**
- **5 eggs**
- **¼ cup milk**
- **¼ teaspoon seasoned salt or salt**
- **Dash pepper**
- **3 slices American cheese, cut into strips**
- **5 thin slices cooked ham, cut into quarters**

Heat oven to 400°F. Bake biscuits as directed on package; keep warm. Meanwhile, melt margarine in medium skillet over medium heat; tilt pan to coat. In small bowl, combine eggs, milk, seasoned salt and pepper; blend well. Pour egg mixture into skillet; reduce heat to low. Cook until eggs are almost set but still moist, stirring occasionally from outside edge to center, allowing uncooked egg to flow to bottom of skillet. Top with cheese strips. Cover tightly. Let stand 2 to 3 minutes or until cheese is melted.

In another skillet, heat ham over low heat until thoroughly heated. To assemble sandwiches, split warm biscuits. Place 2 pieces of ham on bottom half of each biscuit. Spoon egg mixture evenly over ham. Top each with remaining biscuit halves. 10 sandwiches.

NUTRITION INFORMATION

SERVING SIZE: 1 SANDWICH		PERCENT U.S. RDA PER SERVING	
CALORIES	190	PROTEIN	10%
PROTEIN	9 g	VITAMIN A	6%
CARBOHYDRATE	15 g	VITAMIN C	*
FAT	11 g	THIAMINE	10%
CHOLESTEROL	118 mg	RIBOFLAVIN	15%
SODIUM	620 mg	NIACIN	6%
POTASSIUM	170 mg	CALCIUM	8%
		IRON	6%

* Contains less than 2% of the U.S. RDA of this nutrient.

The tangy flavor of this chicken mixture will depend on the brands of barbecue sauce and salsa you use. To complete this sandwich meal, serve it with tortilla chips and cut-up fresh vegetables.

SOUTHWEST BARBECUED CHICKEN SANDWICHES

- **1½ cups shredded cooked chicken***
- **½ cup chunky salsa**
- **½ cup barbecue sauce**
- **2 tablespoons sliced green onions**
- **5 whole grain buns, split, toasted if desired**

In medium saucepan, combine all ingredients except buns; mix well. Cook over low heat 10 minutes to blend flavors, stirring occasionally. Serve on buns. 5 sandwiches.

MICROWAVE DIRECTIONS: In 1½ to 2-quart microwave-safe casserole, combine all ingredients except buns; mix well. Cover. Microwave on HIGH for 4 to 5 minutes or until mixture is thoroughly heated, stirring twice during cooking. Serve on buns.

TIP:

* One 6¾-oz. can chunk chicken, drained and flaked, can be substituted for shredded cooked chicken.

NUTRITION INFORMATION

SERVING SIZE: 1 SANDWICH		PERCENT U.S. RDA PER SERVING	
CALORIES	210	PROTEIN	25%
PROTEIN	17 g	VITAMIN A	6%
CARBOHYDRATE	24 g	VITAMIN C	4%
FAT	5 g	THIAMINE	10%
CHOLESTEROL	39 mg	RIBOFLAVIN	8%
SODIUM	630 mg	NIACIN	25%
POTASSIUM	320 mg	CALCIUM	6%
		IRON	10%

Here is another way to use ***Quick Pasta Sauce*** *(p. 11).*

VEGETABLE-TOPPED ITALIAN SANDWICHES

(pictured on right)

2 tablespoons oil
1½ cups Green Giant® Frozen Broccoli Cuts (from 16-oz. pkg.)
½ cup coarsely chopped onion
1 (4.5-oz.) jar Green Giant® Sliced Mushrooms, drained
1 garlic clove, minced, or ½ teaspoon chopped garlic in oil
2 cups Quick Pasta Sauce (page 11)
4 kaiser rolls, split
6 oz. (1½ cups) shredded mozzarella cheese

Heat oil in medium skillet over medium-high heat. Gradually add frozen broccoli; cook and stir 3 minutes. Reduce heat to medium. Add onion, mushrooms and garlic; cook and stir 4 minutes or until broccoli is tender. Meanwhile, heat pasta sauce in small saucepan.

To assemble sandwiches, place roll halves, cut side up, on ungreased cookie sheet or broiler pan; toast under broiler, if desired. Spoon ¼ cup of the pasta sauce over each roll half. Using slotted spoon, top each with ¼ cup of broccoli mixture and 2 tablespoons of the cheese. Broil 4 to 6 inches from heat 1 to 2 minutes or until cheese is melted. 8 sandwiches.

MICROWAVE DIRECTIONS:
In 1½-quart microwave-safe casserole, combine **1 tablespoon oil**, frozen broccoli, onion, mushrooms and garlic. Cover tightly. Microwave on HIGH for 5 to 6 minutes or until broccoli is crisp-tender, stirring once halfway through cooking. Place pasta sauce in 4-cup microwave-safe measuring cup. Cover with waxed paper. Microwave on HIGH for 5 to 6 minutes or until thoroughly heated, stirring once halfway through cooking. If desired, microwave each roll half on HIGH for 10 to 15 seconds or until warm.

Vegetable-Topped Italian Sandwiches

To assemble sandwiches, place 4 roll halves on microwave-safe plate or platter. Spoon ¼ cup of the pasta sauce over each roll half. Using slotted spoon, top each with ¼ cup of broccoli mixture and 2 tablespoons of the cheese. Microwave on HIGH for 1 to 2 minutes or until cheese is melted. Repeat with remaining roll halves, pasta sauce and cheese.

NUTRITION INFORMATION

SERVING SIZE: 1 SANDWICH		PERCENT U.S. RDA PER SERVING	
CALORIES	240	PROTEIN	20%
PROTEIN	13 g	VITAMIN A	20%
CARBOHYDRATE	23 g	VITAMIN C	25%
FAT	12 g	THIAMINE	15%
CHOLESTEROL	23 mg	RIBOFLAVIN	10%
SODIUM	670 mg	NIACIN	10%
POTASSIUM	340 mg	CALCIUM	20%
		IRON	10%

Chowders, originally made with seafood, are now made with other meats. The Green Giant® frozen vegetable mixture used in this recipe reduces preparation time by eliminating the cleaning and cutting up of vegetables.

NEW ENGLAND HAM AND VEGETABLE CHOWDER

3 tablespoons margarine or butter
½ cup chopped onion
3 tablespoons flour
4 cups milk
1½ cups cubed cooked ham
1 (16-oz.) pkg. Green Giant® American Mixtures™ New England Style Frozen Peas, Potatoes and Carrots
½ teaspoon salt
⅛ teaspoon pepper

Melt margarine in 4-quart saucepan or Dutch oven over medium heat. Add onion; cook and stir until tender. Reduce heat to low. Stir in flour; cook and stir until mixture is smooth and bubbly. Gradually stir in milk. Add remaining ingredients. Bring to a boil over medium heat, stirring frequently. Reduce heat to low; simmer 10 to 15 minutes or until slightly thickened and vegetables are tender, stirring occasionally.
5 (1¼-cup) servings.

NUTRITION INFORMATION

SERVING SIZE: 1-1/4 CUPS		PERCENT U.S. RDA PER SERVING	
CALORIES	310	PROTEIN	30%
PROTEIN	19 g	VITAMIN A	90%
CARBOHYDRATE	29 g	VITAMIN C	25%
FAT	14 g	THIAMINE	40%
CHOLESTEROL	37 mg	RIBOFLAVIN	30%
SODIUM	970 mg	NIACIN	15%
POTASSIUM	660 mg	CALCIUM	25%
		IRON	10%

Children will especially enjoy this quick-to-make mild cheese soup studded with tuna and colorful vegetables. Serve it with warm biscuits and assorted fruit.

CHEESY TUNA VEGETABLE CHOWDER

¼ cup margarine or butter
½ cup chopped onion
¼ cup flour
½ teaspoon dry mustard
⅛ teaspoon pepper
2 cups milk
1 (10½-oz.) can condensed chicken broth
2 cups Green Giant® Frozen Mixed Vegetables (from 16-oz. pkg.)
¼ teaspoon dried marjoram leaves, crushed
4 oz. (1 cup) cubed American cheese
1 (6½-oz.) can tuna packed in water, drained, flaked

Melt margarine in large saucepan over medium heat. Add onion; cook and stir until tender. Reduce heat to low. Stir in flour, dry mustard and pepper; cook and stir until mixture is smooth and bubbly. Gradually stir in milk and broth. Stir in frozen vegetables and marjoram. Bring to a boil over medium heat, stirring occasionally. Reduce heat to low; cover and simmer 3 to 5 minutes or until vegetables are crisp-tender. Add cheese and tuna; heat, stirring gently, until cheese is melted.
4 (1¼-cup) servings.

NUTRITION INFORMATION

SERVING SIZE: 1-1/4 CUPS		PERCENT U.S. RDA PER SERVING	
CALORIES	420	PROTEIN	45%
PROTEIN	28 g	VITAMIN A	100%
CARBOHYDRATE	24 g	VITAMIN C	10%
FAT	24 g	THIAMINE	10%
CHOLESTEROL	43 mg	RIBOFLAVIN	25%
SODIUM	1240 mg	NIACIN	40%
POTASSIUM	650 mg	CALCIUM	35%
		IRON	15%

We've used shredded lettuce for a cool, crunchy addition to this ever-popular sandwich.

CHILI CHEESE DOGS

4 wieners
1 cup Quick and Easy Chili (page 16)
1 cup shredded lettuce
4 wiener buns, split
1 oz. (¼ cup) shredded Cheddar cheese

Place wieners in medium saucepan; cover with water. Simmer 5 to 8 minutes or until thoroughly heated. Meanwhile, in small saucepan cook chili until thoroughly heated, stirring occasionally. Place ¼ cup of the lettuce on each split bun; add wiener. Top each with ¼ cup of the chili and 1 tablespoon of the cheese. Serve immediately. 4 servings.

MICROWAVE DIRECTIONS: Place wieners on microwave-safe plate. Cover with waxed paper. Microwave on MEDIUM for 3 to 4 minutes or until thoroughly heated. Place chili in 1-quart microwave-safe casserole or bowl. Cover with waxed paper. Microwave on HIGH for 3 to 4 minutes or until thoroughly heated, stirring once halfway through cooking. Assemble sandwiches as directed above.

NUTRITION INFORMATION

SERVING SIZE: 1/4 OF RECIPE		PERCENT U.S. RDA PER SERVING	
CALORIES	420	PROTEIN	30%
PROTEIN	19 g	VITAMIN A	10%
CARBOHYDRATE	35 g	VITAMIN C	25%
FAT	22 g	THIAMINE	25%
CHOLESTEROL	49 mg	RIBOFLAVIN	15%
SODIUM	1230 mg	NIACIN	25%
POTASSIUM	540 mg	CALCIUM	10%
		IRON	20%

This soup will make any dinner special. Because wild rice needs 40 to 50 minutes of cooking time, prepare it ahead, then refrigerate (several days) or freeze it until you're ready to use it.

CHICKEN MUSHROOM WILD RICE SOUP

1 tablespoon margarine or butter
2 cups (about 5 oz.) sliced fresh mushrooms
½ cup chopped green onions
3 (14½-oz.) cans chicken broth
2 cups cooked wild rice
1½ cups cut-up cooked chicken or turkey
½ cup coarsely shredded carrot
½ teaspoon poultry seasoning
¼ teaspoon dried marjoram leaves, crushed
1 to 2 tablespoons dry sherry, if desired

Melt margarine in 4-quart saucepan or Dutch oven over medium heat. Add mushrooms and green onions; cover and cook 2 to 3 minutes or until mushrooms release juices. Stir in remaining ingredients except sherry; simmer uncovered 10 minutes, stirring occasionally. Stir in sherry; salt and pepper to taste.
6 (1⅓-cup) servings.

NUTRITION INFORMATION

SERVING SIZE: 1-1/3 CUPS		PERCENT U.S. RDA PER SERVING	
CALORIES	190	PROTEIN	25%
PROTEIN	17 g	VITAMIN A	50%
CARBOHYDRATE	16 g	VITAMIN C	4%
FAT	6 g	THIAMINE	6%
CHOLESTEROL	31 mg	RIBOFLAVIN	15%
SODIUM	710 mg	NIACIN	40%
POTASSIUM	460 mg	CALCIUM	2%
		IRON	8%

Index

MW = MICROWAVE DIRECTIONS, MWO = MICROWAVE DIRECTIONS ONLY

MW = MICROWAVE DIRECTIONS, MWO = MICROWAVE DIRECTIONS ONLY

Skillet Barbecued Pork Chops p. 31, Sunny California Broccoli Toss p. 71

MW = MICROWAVE DIRECTIONS, MWO = MICROWAVE DIRECTIONS ONLY

Nutrition Information

Nutrition Information: Pillsbury recipe analysis is provided per serving or per unit of food and is based on the most current nutritional values available from the United States Department of Agriculture (USDA) and food manufacturers. Each recipe is calculated for number of calories; grams of protein, carbohydrate and fat; and milligrams of cholesterol, sodium and potassium.

Vitamin and mineral levels are stated as percentages of United States Recommended Daily Allowances. RDAs are the dietary standards determined by the U.S. Food and Drug Administration for healthy people. If you are following a medically prescribed diet, consult your physician or registered dietitian about using this nutrition information.

Calculating Nutrition Information: Recipe analysis is calculated on:

- A single serving based on the largest number of servings, or on a specific amount (1 tablespoon) or unit (1 cookie).
- The first ingredient or amount when more than one is listed.
- "If desired" or garnishing ingredients when they are included in the ingredient listing.
- Only the amount of a marinade or frying oil absorbed during preparation.

Using Nutrition Information: The amount of nutrients a person needs is determined by one's age, size and activity level. The following are general guidelines you can use for evaluating your daily food intake:

Calories: 2350
Protein: 45 to 65 grams
Carbohydrates: 340 grams
Fat: 80 grams or less
Cholesterol: 300 milligrams or less
Sodium: 2400 milligrams

A nutritionally balanced diet recommends limiting intake of fat to 30 percent or less of total daily calories. One gram of fat is 9 calories. You can determine the fat content of recipes or products with the following formula:

$$\frac{\text{GRAMS OF FAT PER SERVING} \times 9}{\text{TOTAL CALORIES PER SERVING}} = \text{PERCENT OF CALORIES FROM FAT}$$

$$\text{(Example: } \frac{8 \times 9}{310} = \frac{72}{310} = 22\%\text{)}$$